A Writer's Guide

Beyond Kings & Princesses

Governments for Worldbuilders

Book One of Politics for Worldbuilders
by Oren Litwin

LAGRANGE
BOOKS

Published by Lagrange Books
Visit our website at https://lagrangebooks.com
Contact us at editor@lagrangebooks.com.

This is a work of general reference. No specific reliance should be placed on the material herein for accuracy of facts and figures, or any other purpose.

Cover design and layout by Miriam Albright.
Editing by Gayle Statman.

First Edition

ISBN 978-0-9897230-8-4 (paperback)

BEYOND KINGS & PRINCESSES

Governments for Worldbuilders

More from Lagrange Books

Fantasy Anthologies
Ye Olde Magick Shoppe: Stories of Magic for Sale
*The Wand that Rocks the Cradle: Magical Stories
of Family*

Science-fiction Anthologies
Asteroids! Stories of Space Adventure
(coming soon!)

Short Story Collections
Misha Burnett, *Bad Dreams and Broken Hearts:
The Case Files of Erik Rugar*

Nonfiction
Ron Farina, *Who Will Have My Back*
(coming soon!)

LAGRANGE
BOOKS

For Elisha,
who loves a good story.

Contents

Contents

Introduction

Worldbuilding is fun. Whether you are trying to write a fantasy novel or a sci-fi graphic novel, create a video game, or even run a tabletop adventure, being able to create your own world from scratch is a feeling like no other.

And one of the coolest parts is being able to create your world's politics. Do you want medieval kings and nobles? Intergalactic empires? Tense intrigue in a democracy or oligarchy? To invent your own, brand-new system—like maybe have the ruler be a magical ageless child who likes unicorns, or a system where all political decisions are made by AI? You can do it. You set the rules.

But if that's so—if we as worldbuilders are infinitely free to create what we want—then *why do many political settings look the same?*

The good-hearted queen loved by the commoners, but opposed by a scheming minister. The stout farmhand who arises from humble beginnings to lead a rebellion. The cruel overlord who murders lots of people for kicks, with none to oppose him. You can fill in the blanks, because you've seen it so many times before.

That's not *necessarily* a problem. There are plenty of tried-and-true story archetypes out there that good worldbuilders can shape into fun, gripping stories. And political tropes like farmhand-led rebellions are no different.

Still, story is built on conflict. Conflict often arises from the worldbuilding—and particularly from your setting's politics. (Politics *is* conflict, as we shall see.) And that means that if your *worldbuilding* is using the same tropes as everyone else, then your *conflict* will be like everyone else's—and that means your *story* will be like everyone else's.

Again, not always bad. We each can put our own spin on the classics.

But our settings constrain our stories, and often determine them. A story of dynastic intrigue would look very different in the ancient kingdom of Vampirica than it would in 1950s Chicago. A female mercenary would get a very different reaction in the Asteroid Belt than she would get in medieval England. A story about honor would look very different in colonial America, early-modern Russia, and 1990s Bosnia. Each of these stories can be good, but it might not be the story you want to tell.

Different settings suggest different kinds of stories, different kinds of conflict.

And if you're doing the three-millionth rehash of

Robin Hood or of King Arthur, many types of conflict will seem painfully out of place.

But what if you want something different?

What if you'd rather create a new, fresh political system for your setting? Or what if you want to take an off-the-shelf system, give it your own tweak, and then see what kinds of new stories emerge?

What if, instead of trying to wedge your story into a setting that doesn't quite fit, like telling a story about democratic empowerment set in the Assyrian Empire (hmm… actually that might be kind of fun…), you designed your setting to put maximum emphasis on *your* story conflict?

Wouldn't that be cool?

But wait. Making up your own system is fraught with risks. In the worst case, you could invent a system that just sounds silly because it would fail instantly, like giving dogs the right to vote. And even when you try to do something new, you're apt to accidentally fall into the same patterns as everyone else—because you're steeped in the same narratives as they are. Your first instinct will be to use the same tropes that you've seen other people use.

To do fresh worldbuilding right, wouldn't you need to become an expert in politics?

Not necessarily.

But you do need the right *tools*. Ideally, these are a small set of powerful, flexible concepts that even a newbie can use effectively.

Easy, right? There's lots of writer's tools on the Internet. There are checklists for character design, or plot structure, or even ways to hook the reader on page 1. There have to be some tools for redesigning your setting's politics, right?

I assumed so myself. But when I looked, it seemed that very few worldbuilding resources discuss politics at all. More often, what they discuss is a society's *culture*. Culture is important in politics, of course, but it's not the whole story.

And when a resource did discuss politics, it was usually a detail-oriented checklist: How many earls serve under a baron? How long has the royal dynasty ruled the land, and how many scheming uncles are in the wings? How many legislators are in parliament?

Now this is all useful for nailing down the texture of your society—but *only* once you have the basic concept thought out. It *doesn't* help you choose the basic concept in the first place—nor does it help you understand how your design choices affect your story.

But what if you had a short guide that gave you:

- the most important underlying dilemmas of politics,
- the three fundamental types of societies,
- the four main rivals for political rule,

- rules for how each uses the Tripod of Power to secure its regime,

- the simple rules for not being overthrown, and

- a system for putting it all together, in endless configurations—whether you're creating a monarchy, a democracy, a theocracy, or something else entirely?

Well, rejoice! For that is exactly what you have before you. With the tools in this guide, you will have the power to create all-new settings for the stories *you* want to tell.

I've been working on the *Politics for Worldbuilders* series (of which this guide is Volume 1) since 2013. Participating in the annual National Novel Writing Month for the umpteenth time that year, I was struck yet again by how many people were crying out for help designing their political settings. I knew that I could create what they needed.

Why? I have a PhD in political science. I've taught classes at the U.S. Naval Academy. I've worked in Washington, DC, and seen some of the ugly bits of politics up close.

More than that, I'm a writer and publisher. I've studied what makes a good story for many years, first with excellent teachers and guidebooks, then while writing my own works, and then while putting together edited anthologies from stories that writers like you submitted to Lagrange Books, my imprint.

Not only do I know politics—I also know what's important when writing *stories* about politics. And I can help you apply those principles in your own work.

So read on, brave worldbuilder. Together, we will craft political settings that will make your stories powerful.

Chapter 1: Conflict in Politics

Why use politics in fiction?

Or, put another way, what is it about politics that can generate compelling fiction?

To answer that, first we have to understand what politics *is*.

Think about the phrase "office politics." What does that suggest to you?

People fighting over budgets, or over who gets the next promotion. Cliques of employees scheming to discredit rivals, or to get them fired. Big proposals being shot down, or approved, because of who stands to gain prestige because of them.

What about the opposite of office politics? What would that look like? (Is there such a thing?)

Everything in the office runs smoothly. Teams cooperate to achieve their goals. Big decisions are made based on dispassionate analysis of options, creating consensus, and a focus on the good of the organization.

Mentoring of new talent occurs without favoritism.

I think we would all love to *work* in such an office!

But would we love to *read* about it?

Possibly, if such a gloriously functional office were faced with an outside threat, and needed to unearth new depths of competence to persevere. But notice that we needed to reach *outside* of the office to find conflict, to make the story interesting.

Fiction is conflict. I'm sure you've heard it a million times, but it's still true.

There can be many kinds of conflict: protagonist versus antagonist, versus nature, versus self, *et cetera*. And people have made compelling fiction out of even the most mundane-seeming conflicts—who gets the red stapler, perhaps. But conflict there must be.

And conflict is the very *heart* of politics. But conflict over what?

Different people have given different answers over time.

Early political scientists often defined "politics" as something like, "**The authoritative allocation of scarce goods.**"

As a definition, this isn't very good. It suggests some bureaucrat sitting in a central office, dispassionately calculating the chocolate ration; certainly a *kind* of politics, but hardly the only kind. But it still directs our attention to a few points:

- "Goods" suggests that people *already* know what they want, what they value.

- "Scarce goods" implies that some people will get what they want, and others won't. They might have to make do with less, or go without entirely. Those people will not be happy, and will want to *change* the outcome—or the status quo.

- "Authoritative" highlights the importance of *authority*: the sense that some people or some commands *ought* to be followed. In other words, a key aspect of politics is about leadership and obedience, and how that comes about.

Already we have a rich set of concepts for fiction. Let's look at an example of their use.

Paolo Bacigalupi's book *The Water Knife* features a dystopian near-future Southwest United States in which water is scarce, and the key violent conflicts in the book revolve around the acquisition by ruthless oligarchs of legal rights to water. Those who try to access water illegally are hunted and killed by state-sanctioned assassins, who also dabble in unsanctioned murder to protect the interests of their bosses.

However, the major plot elements are driven by *legal ownership* of water, not mere violent possession of it. If there were not a legal framework governing who gets to have water and who does not, there would be no real stakes in the story and no hope for the villain's eventual comeuppance.

This is an excellent example of where *authority* matters in the allocation of scarce goods.

Note that a "scarce good" might be physical, like food or land or gold; but it might be something else, like prestige or status, or first place in a competition, or a romantic partner. It might be a privilege like wearing a special kind of hat. It might be the top bunk in a prison cell. It might be the right to apprentice under a powerful and reclusive archmage. All these things can be fought over; and when that fight is settled by questions of authority and power, then it enters the realm of politics.

This book is meant to be practical. Every time we have a new concept, you'll be given exercises for using the concept in fiction. You can pass over them if you like and just read the book straight; but then you'll be missing a lot of the value of this book.

Exercise

1. Take an existing fictional setting, either yours or someone else's. What are the "scarce goods" in that setting? What makes them scarce? How do people know they are "good"? (Remember that the goods need not be physical.)

2. How are the goods "allocated"? By whom? Who gets them, and who does not?

3. By what authority are the goods allocated? If the have-nots

are unhappy, does anything stop them from trying to change things—even violently?

4. Where did this authority come from? What would happen if the source of that authority changed? What if a new authority were to arise?

Now, let's say that we're starting a brand-new setting from scratch. This is Step One in designing a world to tell the story you want to tell. Don't think we're chiseling anything in stone; we're still at the "throwing stuff at the wall" stage here. Don't feel constrained by your answers; this is just to suggest some possibilities. Anything can change later. Explore the space.

1. For this exercise, we assume that you already have an idea of the themes you want to write about. What are they?

2. Do any of these themes suggest conflict over scarce goods?

3. Who has the "good" already? How?

4. Who wants the "good"? Why don't they have it?

5. Do any of these ideas resonate with the story you want to tell?

We mentioned that our first definition of politics assumes that people already know what they value—that values are a given. But we know very well from our own world that *different* values are a key driver of conflict.

Is abortion an act of personal autonomy, or an act of murder? Should marijuana be legal? Does God exist, and if so, what does She want? (Did you get annoyed when I said "She"? Why? What if I had said "He"?)

This book is not about those questions.

But none of those questions has a "logical" answer that can be worked out like a math problem. The way you answer each question is going to depend on the values you hold. And if people disagree on their fundamental values, there is no way to permanently resolve the conflicts between them.

But where did those values come from?

According to some, they come from politics. These people would add another definition of politics as, **"The authoritative determination of values."**

In other words, an authority figure got up and told people that going to college, or exposing crippled infants on a mountainside, or working for a boss, or giving to the United Way, or sacrificing human prisoners to the sun-god, was *the right thing to do*.

And that objecting to these values was *the wrong thing to do*.

Now, we should be a little bit skeptical here. If a county judge were to say that cocaine should be given out free to high-schoolers, most people would laugh.

Why? Because we don't believe that a low-level judge has the *right* to change our values so radically, by fiat.

If the president of the United States said that marijuana should be legalized, on the other hand, some people would cheer and others would object. And on the margin, a few people who were unsure might be swayed to believe that yes, marijuana should be legalized after all.

And what if a prophet were to emerge, speaking on behalf of the moon-goddess Eithi, and saying that Eithi now demands that her worshippers wear only white robes and drink only clear water?

Well, if you don't follow Eithi in the first place, you wouldn't care; but if you did, then this prophet might well have the power to change your practices.

Could such a change lead to conflict? You bet!

Take Robert Heinlein's *Stranger in a Strange Land*, one of the seminal works of the 1960s counterculture movement. The titular stranger, Michael Valentine Smith, was raised on Mars and so has very different cultural values than most of humanity. As he teaches these values to others, his growing influence sparks a violent struggle with the existing dominant religion—which considers Smith's views to be heresy.

Note also that if your values change, what you consider a "good" might change as well. Most Americans enjoy eating meat despite its relative expense compared to other foods; but vegans wouldn't try it if you paid *them*.

Exercise

1. What are the major values or ethical beliefs of your setting?

2. Which of them create conflict for your characters?

3. How might these values change?

4. Does anyone want to change any of these beliefs? With what authority, or by what means?

5. Does anyone want that belief to remain as it is?

6. What might that person do to defend the status quo?

Values can direct behavior; but they can also *justify* behavior.

And for many people, values can be remarkably flexible as the need arises. As the apocryphal politician put it, "Those are my principles, and if you don't like them—I have others."

Sometimes, values can be nothing more than a language people use to convince others (and sometimes themselves) that what they are *already doing* is great, and they don't need to change. Indeed, values can be used as a weapon, to excuse what would otherwise be crimes.

And in many cases, values don't even enter into the discussion—nor does the authoritative allocation of scarce goods, per se, unless we stretch the definition of "goods" to the breaking-point. Sometimes, political conflict is about nothing more than naked ambition.

Which brings us to Leon Trotsky's famously cynical definition of politics (which he adapted from an in-passing quip of Lenin's): **"the question of *who* and *whom*."**

What does that mean?

As Trotsky explains in *Their Morals and Ours,* politics is about the endless struggle of social groups for power over each other—to determine *who* can enforce its will against *whom*.

This needn't even be about who gets "scarce goods" or about who gets to impose moral values, though it certainly can be. Rather, it's about raw power—perhaps power for the sake of accomplishing other, later goals, but in the worst case it can be power for its own sake. Appeals to values, analysis of policies, appeals to shared humanity or moral principles or whatever, all of these are merely rationalizations for the will to power.

We all know examples of the politician who will say anything, support anything, in order to win election. And then in the next election, the very same politician will switch policies wholesale! All that seems to matter is which way the wind blows, and how to ensure access to power.

Perhaps the crowning literary example is George Orwell's *1984*. As explained in the fictional Emmanuel Goldstein book *The Theory and Practice of Oligarchical Collectivism*, Nazism and Communism both used ideological appeals that the inner party members did not truly believe, in order to attract followers and gain power.

The ultimate development of that trend, for Orwell, was a Party that explicitly believed in nothing but power itself, power as the highest end.

It gets worse. One of the great tragedies of the world is this: the will to power often coexists with more noble goals—and often corrupts them. As an apocryphal quote inspired by Eric Hoffer puts it, "Every great cause begins as a movement, becomes a business, and ultimately degenerates into a racket."

Exercise

1. Go back over the conflicts that you sketched out in your setting. For each one, take each faction of the conflict, one at a time, and answer from its perspective:

   A. Who is the "good guy"? Who is the "bad guy"?

   B. What does this perspective justify doing to the "bad guys"? What does it justify doing to "collaborators" or "traitors" among the "good guys"?

   C. Who needs power or leadership in order to achieve the goals of this faction? Whose power is legitimate?

   D. What in this perspective might justify a power struggle among the leadership?

2. Suppose that you don't care at all about who is right or wrong—you just want wealth or power. How might joining either side give you what you want? What about associating with both sides?

3. Suppose you begin as a true believer. What temptations will there be to compromise your beliefs for the sake of personal gain?

4. Do any of the ideas you've sketched out resonate with the story you want to tell?

So we have conflict over scarce goods, conflict over values, and conflict over power itself. Politics usually has aspects of all three at once.

For fiction writers, politics offers a treasure trove of possibilities. Not only could we get many individual ideas for story conflicts—we can build even more powerful conflicts by layering the different aspects of political conflict on top of each other, and on top of other conflicts in your story.

Consider a standard romance plot, Girl Wants Guy and Can't Have Him. Why not? Maybe her parents disapprove. Fine. But why?

Maybe the Guy is in the Orange faction, and the Girl's family are staunch Blues. Maybe the Girl's father is trying to become the leader of the Blue faction, and would lose face if his daughter was seen running around with a hated Orange.

And maybe the father wants the leadership because the existing leader of the Blues is planning a massacre of the Orange faction. And the father, horrified, wants to stop it however possible.

And maybe the Girl has a jilted suitor who is *also* vying for the leadership of the Blues, and would love to knock his rival (the Girl's father) down a peg. Or maybe just shoot him, and his whole family, if he can get away with it.

And this doesn't even consider what could be happening on the Guy's side of things!

By layering several different political lenses on top of the original plot, we've taken a conventional story and packed it full of tension, high stakes, intrigue, and agonizing dilemmas. Pretty good, huh?

Now it's your turn. How could you use the three aspects of political conflict we discussed to improve your story?

Politics can be a powerful tool in the writer's toolbox. The next step is to make sure we know how to use that tool most effectively.

If you've gotten this far, it's because you want an alternative to the Robin Hood/French Revolution pastiches that have been done to death. And in the chapters to follow, we will be looking at some key concepts for how governments work that can give you the groundwork for telling new and awesome stories.

A caveat:

I am *not* arguing that This Is The Only Way to Write About Politics. If, after you read this book, you decide that you actually want to tell stories about the Fairy Princess Toomi and her quest for the Magical Crown of Crowniness, that is totally fine. Really.

I do not insist on slavish mimicry of real life for its own sake. That's why it's fiction. But I *do* think that we can learn a lot from real life, that many authors would expand their range by learning new things.

This is about telling *stories*. And giving you the tools to tell the story *you* want to tell.

Even if it's different from any other story you've seen, any other setting. Especially then!

With the concepts to come, you will have the raw material to break out of existing conventions—if you want to. And if not, that's fine too. You'll be able to take those conventions and give them even more punch.

First we learn our tools. Then we can decide how to use them.

Onward.

Chapter 2: Introduction to Class Conflict

There are many kinds of conflict between people, from two suitors vying over the same romantic partner to two coworkers who get on each other's nerves. But for a conflict to be *political,* it has to involve *several* people at minimum, not just two.

You can certainly have a political conflict *between* two people—rival princesses, say, struggling over the throne. But what are they *really* struggling over? The loyalty of other people besides themselves.

And that means that many other people have to be taken into account: what they want from a queen, what might sway them toward one princess or the other, and the relationships between powerful figures and each of the rival princesses.

This is complicated enough when the audience of a political struggle is just a few people—say, other members of a family, or a small social club.

But if you want to discuss large numbers of people—the population of a city, or a country, or a galaxy—it can seem paralyzing.

There is a way, however, to streamline conflicts without losing their scope: thinking about **groups of people** as political actors.

What makes a set of individuals into a group? What binds them together? What interests do they share? What distinguishes them from people outside the group? What internal tensions might they have, or conflicting loyalties? What other groups are they in conflict with, and why?

A full discussion of all these issues would take another book (and that's the plan; keep your eye out for future volumes of *Politics for Worldbuilders*). For our purposes, we want to focus on a type of group conflict that's vitally important for the question of who rules a country: class conflict.

Now let's pause right here. I *don't* mean the common model of upper, middle, and lower classes that people often fixate on. The truth is, "class" is a conceptual construct. You, the observer, decide how to categorize people into classes—and you can assign the same person into many different classes, depending on what you're trying to get at in your analysis.

You could lump a bunch of people into a single lower class, or you could distinguish between itinerant artists, day laborers, retail salesfolk, and panhandlers—each of which behaves very differently, and each of which has different interests.

(The economist Joseph Schumpeter even identified a class of "resentful intellectuals," who he thought were dangerous to society! See the "Further Reading" section.)

So let's briefly define *class*, for our purposes, as "**a group of people with shared interests, background, training, or beliefs that lead them to behave in similar ways and to want similar things.**" (If you prefer, you could use the term "interest group" to mean nearly the same thing.)

Each of the shared characteristics listed could lead to interesting stories. But let's narrow in on shared interests— because *class interests* are a powerful factor in politics.

Imagine a small nomadic band of hunter-gatherers, living a carefree existence in the wild hill country—let's call them the Pandu. They own little property aside from the weapons and tools they carry and the clothing they wear. Let's even suppose that they practice free love, and that children are raised communally (just to exclude one possible source of conflict from our discussion). Finally, imagine that everyone performs the same jobs: hunting, foraging, making clothing and tools, raising children, and making decorative jewelry that looks pretty (we can call these "prestige goods").

One might think that the Pandu ought to be the perfect egalitarian society, without conflict over possessions or political power. (And actual foraging societies often tend to be nearly egalitarian, for reasons we'll discuss in Chapter 4). Still, they are not perfectly egalitarian, even if there are no hard class divisions. Why?

Let's say that some Pandu are better at hunting or foraging than others. Such "Good Hunters" manage to gather enough food in a shorter time; then they can spend more time creating jewelry, or other prestige goods. Or they can gather *extra* food and trade it with others for their prestige goods.

Over time, they will accumulate more jewelry than less-skilled hunters. At this point, jewelry starts to be not just pretty shiny things, but a sign of hunting skill. Good Hunters will start to attract more intimate partners because of their greater prestige, or simply with gifts of food or jewelry; lesser hunters will lose out, in relative terms.

If the story ends here, we would have a society shot through with simmering tensions and periodic fits of jealousy-driven violence. But the Pandu would still be broadly classless, because both Good Hunters and average hunters have the same *interests*. They hunt the same game, gather the same foods, and value the same goods.

Now imagine that successful hunters had the right to eat their prey's hearts, which grant magical powers and even greater hunting skill. Suddenly, we have a "rich-get-richer" scenario: Good Hunters would soon outstrip their less-skilled rivals, becoming a class in themselves that eventually possesses far more food, prestige, and social attractiveness than the "lower" class. The lower class could still feed itself, but would lack prestige and social standing, and likely intimate partners as a result—and would have no way to catch up, at least not through hunting skill.

Does this create a true class division? Good and average hunters still have the same interests and value the same things. But on the other hand, the average hunters now have a new desire: some way to assert their own value, to balance the scales with the Good Hunters. If ignored, this new interest will probably lead to even more episodes of violence against arrogant Good Hunters.

So here, the average hunters could indeed be considered their own class. And managing the tensions between these two classes will be an important part of Pandu daily life. But as long as interclass jealousy is kept under control, perhaps by social rituals that periodically erase class distinctions, the Pandu band will remain unified. Since the two classes both engage in hunting, they still value the same kinds of things.

Now suppose that the less-successful hunters, recognizing that they cannot compete at hunting, decide to abandon hunting entirely. Instead they become Farmers, so that they can win prestige and intimate partners of their own. Suppose they are successful, and produce as much food on average as the Good Hunters do, achieving a broadly comparable social status. How does this change the picture?

For one thing, while the Good Hunters would continue their nomadic lifestyle, following the game as the seasons shift, Farmers suddenly are tied to a fixed plot of land. Even if they can travel during fallow seasons or between the planting and harvest time, they would have to return to their plots of land to harvest their crop. Even if they plant multiple crops in multiple locations and circulate between them, they are now less mobile than before.

That means that while Good Hunters have an *interest* in moving around, Farmers have an *interest* in staying close to their land. These interests are potentially in conflict.

What's more, Farmers have to feed themselves somehow while their crop is growing. They might borrow food from fellow Pandu, promising to repay them at the harvest. Likely, they would borrow from the Good Hunters, since hunting can be done even between harvests. But maybe the Good Hunters take advantage of the new situation. Maybe they demand back more food than they lent, in order to gain a profit.

This presents a second clash of interests. Good Hunters want their rights as lenders upheld, and perhaps to gain additional privileges in the process; Farmers would want to defend themselves against such privileges, or even to cancel their debts!

So now we have two groups of people, of roughly equal wealth and social standing, yet with very different behaviors and interests. They are two separate classes, with *conflicting* class interests.

So which class will the Pandu band favor? That's where politics come in. The outcome will be influenced by religious beliefs, the personalities of the leaders of the band and of each class, and a host of other factors; but at any time, the band will be pulled in two directions, and reconciling those strains will be a challenge. In the worst case, the band might pull apart entirely, with Good Hunters and Farmers going their separate ways.

What we've just seen is that class is a powerful tool to think about conflict between groups. We authors can use class conflict to efficiently organize the major political conflicts of our stories.

For example, in John Steinbeck's *The Grapes of Wrath*, everything in the story is fundamentally built around the class conflict between California landowners, who want a pool of cheap agricultural labor, and the migrant workers from the Midwest, who want opportunity and decent pay. The behavior of every individual in the story is conditioned by the expectations created by this class conflict—the workers shuttle between jobs looking for enough income to survive, while the landowners imagine that workers who demand better pay are merely "agitating Reds" (which in Steinbeck's case was literally true!).

One crucial point is that the different types of rulers—kings, queens, warlords, prime ministers, whatever—all depend on supporters, and those supporters will have class interests that the ruler must satisfy. (Or the ruler can create brand-new class interests by restructuring society by force—which you can read about in Book Two of this series, *Tyranny for Worldbuilders*.)

So when we think about who's the boss in our stories, part of that question is going to be, "Boss over which classes? And how does the boss account for his or her class interests? And which classes oppose the boss, and why?"

Exercise

1. Take a look at *A Song of Ice and Fire,* by George R.R. Martin. What are the major classes in the setting?

2. What are their class interests? Are any of those interests in conflict? Spend at least ten minutes listing as much as you can.

3. How might each class advance its interests by harming another class?

4. Does class conflict play any role in the story? Does it play any role in the interests, beliefs, or histories of the characters?

5. Does the ending have any implications for class interests? Do any classes have their interests change? How might that affect the future?

6. Take an existing setting you are working on. Go through questions 1-5 above. Did any new ideas come to you? Do any of these ideas seem to work well with your story?

With this brief overview of class analysis, we are now ready to look at probably the single most important problem for any society—the reconciling of wealth and power. In the next chapter we'll go over this in detail, and how you can use this fraught conflict in your stories.

Further Reading

Peter Gourevitch, *Politics in Hard Times*. (A great book in general, this is useful here for his description of different and conflicting interest groups or classes.)

Albert Jay Nock, *Our Enemy, the State*. (This is another example of unexpected class divisions.)

Joseph Schumpeter, *Capitalism, Socialism, and Democracy*. (This is interesting in many ways, such as his critique of Marxist economics and his hugely influential discussion of *creative destruction*; but as far as this chapter is concerned, the important part is his discussions of class analysis in Chapter 2, "Marx the Sociologist" and Chapter 13, "Growing Hostility.")

Chapter 3: Social Orders: Overview

Suppose there were two people stuck on a desert island. One of them has a crate of food; the other has a gun. What do you think is going to happen next?

Very shortly, the person with the gun is going to "own" the food as well; the other person might be dead, or might be reduced to the level of a slave. (In the immortal words of Clint Eastwood, "You see in this world there's two kinds of people, my friend: those with loaded guns, and those who dig. You dig.")

This is probably *the* fundamental problem in politics: how to reconcile wealth with violence, or power.

(Violence and power are not the same thing, as Hannah Arendt noted; see "Further Reading." But for our immediate purposes, they're close enough.)

Throughout history, people with little wealth but a high capacity for violence have used that violence to take others' wealth, either through sheer banditry or by setting themselves up as a ruler and charging taxes (which can amount to the same thing; see "Further Reading").

Conversely, people with a lot of wealth but little power have used their wealth to gain power—if only in self-defense!

And this dynamic has played out throughout history, in endless cycles of bloodshed and misery.

What this means is that to have a stable, functioning society, you need to somehow answer this fundamental question: **How can wealth and power coexist with each other in society, without breaking down into violence?**

To put it bluntly, what factors stop the wealthy from either being plundered by the powerful, or else using their wealth to take power themselves? (Assuming they don't!)

How you answer this question for your own setting is going to play a powerful role in your stories. And there is no "right" answer.

In the real world, the scholars North, Wallis, and Weingast (who we'll call "NWW") have identified three ways of harmonizing wealth and power, which they call *social orders*. (The next three chapters will largely be based on their work.)

In a fictional setting with fantastical elements, you might use one of the three social orders, or you might design your own—once you understand the principles involved.

This is where things get *really* cool.

Money and power are some of the biggest drivers for conflict of all kinds.

And designing your setting to emphasize the precise conflict you want to write about is a powerful tool in the toolbox. So let's get to it, starting with NWW's discussion of the real world and then applying the principles to your writing.

NWW's social orders are:

- the *foraging* social order,
- the *limited-access* or *natural* social order, and
- the *open-access* social order.

Let's translate that into more concrete terms:

Foraging is the more trendy modern term for hunter-gathering.

Limited-access means autocratic governments as they have existed throughout history, with all privileges and rights stemming from the ruler. (This includes many nominal democracies, as we'll discuss.)

Open-access refers to the rare combination of modern liberal democracy and a relatively free economy; both are important.

We'll go through the details of each social order in the next three chapters, but here it is in a nutshell:

- In the *foraging order*, the society is largely egalitarian: most people have roughly equal wealth and power, so there is little danger of a massive conflict between haves and have-nots.

- In the *limited-access order*, the answer is simply that those with power end up taking the wealth, and those with wealth buy access to power—and the ruling class then shuts everyone else out. This system depends on a delicate balance of power between the great actors and their wealth; if anyone suddenly becomes a tempting target for violence, whether because of new wealth or military weakness, the society is in great danger of civil war.

- In the *open-access order*, free political competition and free economic competition each work to keep the order from breaking down. But the system depends on free access; if class boundaries start to harden, if access to economic opportunities or investment capital or a major party's nomination to office become tightly restricted, the society is in danger of backsliding into the limited-access order.

In a fantastical world, you could imagine other factors to separate wealth from power.

For example, perhaps in your world magical skill depends on a strict discipline of asceticism; mages who indulge in physical luxuries soon lose their edge.

Or perhaps the most powerful weapons in the galaxy are built from rare crystals, and the few examples are under the jealous control of the Imperial Regiments (who are cybernetically barred from being bribed).

You can develop your own examples once you know what elements to look for. First, though, I strongly suggest you read the next three chapters all the way through. The better you understand *why* real social orders work, the more convincing your fantastical one will be.

With that, we begin with the foraging band.

Further Reading

Hannah Arendt, *On Violence*. (This is a brilliant essay on the nature of political power—getting people to "act in concert"—and how it is very different from mere violence.)

North, Wallis, and Weingast, *Violence and Social Orders*. (We will be summarizing this book in the next chapters, but we'll regrettably not discuss NWW's fascinating history of how liberal democracy first emerged.)

Mancur Olson, *Power and Prosperity*. (Pay special attention to the first chapter, in which the Nobel Prize-winning economist discusses the metaphor of governments as "stationary bandits.")

Chapter 4: Social Orders: The Foraging Band

Let's return to our friends the Pandu, and imagine that they are all still nomadic hunters and gatherers. The Pandu have few possessions—only what they are able to carry. Some people might have more jewelry or other valuables, but not all that much more than anyone else. There is a limit to how wealthy one can get, since one has have to carry one's own goods and is always on the move. Thus, material inequality is relatively low.

(If they have domesticated livestock, this changes— individuals might own few or many cattle, and the level of potential inequality becomes much greater. This is so even if they remain nomadic.)

Similarly, each Pandu's capacity for violence is roughly the same as any other's—supposing that they all have similar weapons, such as bone knives and spears. Such weapons are fairly easy to make and use, so everyone would have them and there would be no imbalance in "firepower." Individual Pandu might be stronger or weaker, but again, there is a limit to how strong one can be. A strong Pandu warrior might be able to fight two weaker ones at once, but not twenty.

(If some people have special, powerful weapons or equipment, or even magic, this changes as well. If I have a bone knife and you have a bronze sword, or thick leather armor, or both, or an M-16 rifle, you suddenly have an advantage.)

Since there is little inequality and little difference in power between members of the Pandu, we have the conditions that tend towards an *egalitarian* society.

This is also the distinguishing mark of the *foraging* social order. The problem of "wealth vs. power" is resolved because there is little imbalance between a person's wealth and his or her power, and little opportunity to increase one's power and wealth at others' expense. All members of the foraging band are roughly as strong and wealthy as each other; if one person tries to increase personal power illegitimately, the others will simply band together to defeat that member.

And it needn't be through violence, though that remains an ever-present option. The other means that egalitarian bands use to control their members are primarily social, starting with group norms against the accumulation of wealth. Egalitarian societies tend to value their equality, expect members to behave in ways that sustain it, and will disapprove of people who threaten to disrupt it.

Sometimes, the weight of such disapproval is enough to sustain a broadly egalitarian society even where larger inequality is possible, like in an agricultural village. But the balance is more delicate there, and the norms are constantly under threat. (Such cases are really good settings for story conflict!)

Dealing with Inequality

One of the ways egalitarianism is often enforced is through mandatory gift-giving, or public feasting. In exchange for social acceptance and prestige, a wealthy band member will be expected to dissipate that wealth with gifts to others, or by hosting a feast. (There is an amusing parallel between such expectations and the expectations placed on premodern English aristocrats, including the Jane Austen variety, as we will see in Chapter 8.)

But sometimes a band member will ignore these social expectations, try to accumulate wealth or power, and thus pose a threat to the group. If it's a bad threat, this violator might end up being killed outright; trying to lord it over an egalitarian band is a risky business! But short of that, other band members will resort to what James C. Scott (see "Further Reading") calls "weapons of the weak."

It begins with malicious gossip, targeted at the violator. (Remember that the egalitarian band is your main social world; reputation in the band can be life or death!) Then the violator might experience petty acts of uncooperation from the others.

If that doesn't work, the other band members will escalate to explicit public disapproval. If even that doesn't do the trick, the violator may face actual political opposition and the threat of punishment, or even suffer magical curses from enemies (yes, this is a thing in real foraging bands). And again, there's always the option to use violence if other sanctions don't work.

Exercise

Let's say you have an idea for a story that involves a society of people who don't have a fixed home. Perhaps they are wandering cattle-herders, or perhaps they forage for roots and berries in the jungle, or perhaps they are wandering space-gypsies who survive off of volatile gases that their spaceships harvest with ramscoops.

1. Spend a few minutes and list five possible reasons why your band chooses not to have a fixed home. (You don't have to use all five in the actual story. Brainstorm.)

2. What forms of wealth might be different between people? Try to list at least three. Does a given form of wealth tend to be dissipated over time, via feasting or gifting or divisions between heirs or another means? Or does it build on itself?

3. How does the band handle internal conflict? Are there mechanisms for doing this? Would conflict threaten to tear apart the band? What is at stake?

4. Why might outsiders come into conflict with your band? List five possible reasons. ("We raid their settlements and take slaves and plunder" is an acceptable reason! So is "They

want to wear our sparkly purple skin as trophies." What else?)

5. Why does having a wandering band fit in this story? What aspect of such a band fits the theme or the conflict?

Egalitarianism's End

But sometimes, a band member *does* manage to accumulate power. Usually, it's a long process that might take generations. Let's see how:

Foraging bands are often broadly egalitarian, but not *perfectly* egalitarian. Usually, they will have members who are viewed as informal leaders. They might be older, or wiser, or better hunters, and the others look up to them. They might be asked to settle disputes, or make decisions for the band, or lead them in battle or the hunt.

Over time, some of these roles might become formalized. It needn't be in a *single* leader; often, particular families will each have unique privileges, such as the right to carry a sacred object or the right to lead the hunt. But frequently there will indeed be a single leader, who will become a "big man" (as the anthropologists call it—and barring magic or some other equalizer of the sexes, in a dangerous setting it *will* be a man).

The big man is not yet personally wealthy; indeed, because of the expectations placed on him he might be the poorest member of the band! His main economic role is to redistribute wealth from those who have it to those who need it, by taking customary gifts from band members and then giving out his own gifts. Any possessions he has might be demanded of him by band members. But he still has prestige and the privilege to take gifts from the band, and his position will probably be hereditary.

A canny big man might build a group of supporters by enriching them with gifts, especially weapons that make them more powerful than the others. (For example, Danish chiefs in the Early Bronze Age were able to control the trade in rare bronze swords, distributing these powerful weapons to their supporters; see Timothy Earle in "Further Reading.") When the time is right, he will use their support to enrich himself as well, becoming a true "chief" and essentially creating a state regime, establishing a hierarchy of power and wealth.

This hierarchy, and the role of the chief in determining who is favored, is a hallmark of the *limited-access* or *natural* social order. We will look at it in detail in the next chapter.

The Nuclear Option

If a new chief is consolidating power—or if there is some other social conflict within the group that cannot be tolerated—group members do have one final response: to split away from the group and go off on their own in a smaller band. In the literature, this is called "fission." And even if actual fission is rare, the threat of people leaving the group can be a powerful restraint on the more grandiose plans of would-be chiefs. If they push too hard, they could end up having no people left to rule!

But for leaving to be effective, you need to have somewhere to go. As a general rule, it seems that freedom is best defended by people having *options*: in this case, a frontier to escape to.

Peasants in Southeast Asia could escape cruel landlords by fleeing to the forests; Americans in the big East Coast cities could escape corrupt political machines by moving to the open West (see Scott, *The Art of Not Being Governed*).

But if there is nowhere to go—say, you're surrounded by desert or backed up against the sea, or faced by foreign invaders—then a would-be despot will have more leverage over you. It does not seem an accident that the earliest centralized states tended to be in places that were hard to escape from—such as the fertile Nile River Valley, surrounded by desert.

The same concept could apply to other types of control. For example, in the modern world our identities are exhaustively tracked by the government, and it is harder to "escape" such tracking and control than it used to be. Similarly, if your setting featured magical means of control, it might not be possible to escape a new ruler even if you have access to a frontier.

(The topic of control and information is hugely important, and I will be discussing it in much more detail in the next installment of the *Politics for Worldbuilders* series. Check out the sneak preview at the end of this book!)

Exercise

1.   What special status might someone in the band (or some family) have that others do not? Try to list at least three, remembering that not all special statuses need be in the same family. (For example, one family might be war leaders, another might be shamans, another might have the hereditary right to guard the Sacred Hospitality Blanket, and so on.) How might such status be gained or lost?

2.   How might that status be exploited or increased over time?

3.   What changes might give some people more power or wealth? Are there new weapons, or new technology, or new knowledge or skills that allow someone to gain an advantage over others?

4.   How might the others respond? Do they have social or magical resources to restrain an upstart? Could they respond with violence?

5.   In the worst case, is it possible to leave the group? What factors make it more likely? What factors make it less likely?

6.   Do any of these ideas resonate with your story?

We spent a lot of time on egalitarian bands because they provide the baseline for human experience. Our species evolved in such bands, and our instincts of morality and fairness are powerfully shaped by them.

And these attitudes persist in some form, even in more hierarchical settings. Powerful and wealthy people throughout history were expected to be *patrons* of the poorer people around them, providing support and protection, who in turn would become their *clients*. You can think of feudalism as an explicit form of such *patron-client* relationships, but these relationships exist in almost any setting.

For example, in Southeast Asia, landowners would often take a large percentage of the harvest from their sharecroppers, but would be expected to provide food to them if harvests were poor. If food became scarce and people were desperate, yet the wealthy and powerful refused to support the poor, they would often risk being lynched in a peasant uprising! (See James C. Scott, *The Moral Economy of the Peasant*, in "Further Reading.")

In the next chapter, we will look at the most common social order in human history: the natural state.

Further Reading

Timothy Earle, *How Chiefs Come to Power*. (This is a great discussion of archaeological data from Denmark, Hawaii, different locations in South America, and elsewhere trying to determine how states emerged out of less hierarchical societies.)

David Graeber, *Debt: The First 5,000 Years*. (Much of his overall argument about debt is sloppy and in a few places deceptive, but it's still worth considering; and his anthropology of gift-giving is useful here.)

Marshall Sahlins, *Stone Age Economics*. (This is one of the classic discussions of how foraging bands work, and how they were "the original affluent society." James C. Scott's *The Art of Not Being Governed* can be viewed as a sequel.)

James C. Scott, *The Moral Economy of the Peasant* and *Weapons of the Weak*, and *The Art of Not Being Governed*. (*Moral Economy* completely changed my own view of the world. Anything Scott writes is highly recommended.)

Michael Taylor, *Community, Anarchy, and Liberty*. (This discusses the spectrum between egalitarian bands, "big men" tribes, chiefdoms, and true states.)

Chapter 5: Social Orders: The "Natural" State

We mentioned in Chapter 3 that a *social order* is a particular arrangement of society that can reconcile the temptations of power and wealth, so that things don't break down into an orgy of banditry and murder. In the *foraging band*, this was easy enough: everyone has roughly equal power and wealth, so there is little temptation to try to get more by force.

But we saw that one can amass power even in a formerly egalitarian band, and become a chief. This is done by gaining loyal supporters, manipulating prestige, and taking advantage of your control over wealth (aside from the creation of a ruling ideology, which will be important in Chapter 7).

Thus, we come to the *natural state*, or the *limited-access order*: the single most common form of social organization in our written history.

In the natural state, the problem of power and wealth is solved quite simply: those with power get the wealth.

Conversely, those with a lot of wealth either get squeezed by those in power, or they use their wealth to gain power as well.

How is this done? A major feature of the natural state is that there are no general *rights* among the populace—and particularly, no right to engage in politics or in commerce. Instead, specific *privileges* to do so are given by the ruler, and only to the ruler's favored supporters or their hangers-on.

This is why we call it *limited-access*.

Taking the feudal example, if you are not a member of the nobility, your freedoms are tightly constrained. Depending on what time period we are talking about, you may not be allowed to leave your lord's land or to carry weapons. You certainly couldn't marry a noble. And while you might be a petty vendor in the marketplace without much fear, if you wanted to become an artisan or merchant you would have to join a royal guild. Joining an unsanctioned guild might be considered treason!

Until only a few hundred years ago, if an Englishman wanted to form a corporation he needed to petition the Crown for a royal charter, and pay handsomely for the privilege. These charters were rarely granted, and usually only to members of the nobility.

Most of the original American colonies were first established under such royal charters, and the English aristocrats who held the charters hoped to establish a feudal system here until they realized how easily colonists could run away from poor treatment and join the American Indians! (See *Conceived in Liberty*, in "Further Reading." Recall our mention of "fission" in the previous chapter.)

In Communist or Fascist states, even such mundane organizations as chess clubs needed to be approved by the state. Being a member of an unauthorized organization was grounds for suspicion, and could get you thrown in prison. Organizations are sources of power, and all power needed to be under the state's control.

Limiting access to power is easy to understand. Yet why limit *business* opportunities to your supporters if you are a ruler? The first reason is the obvious one: you like money, your supporters do as well, and you want to reward them for their support and keep them loyal to you.

But more fundamentally, the natural state depends on a fragile balancing-act between power and wealth. If someone has more power than wealth, he is likely to resent his lack, and think that a little violence is a great way to get wealthier. If someone has more wealth than power, she is likely to attract vultures who want that wealth and know they have a good chance of getting it by force.

And if someone *outside* of the ruler's circle of supporters becomes wealthy or powerful, it poses a grave threat to the ruling regime.

North, Wallis, and Weingast (NWW) found that during good times, autocracies tended to have *stronger* economic performance than democracies. Why then did democracies tend to do better in the long run? Because autocracies were prone to coups and civil wars—and the destruction and death caused during these episodes tended to erase all of their earlier gains.

Any time someone gets too wealthy, the ruler of a natural state is implicitly threatened. And so is social order generally. If someone else is able to reward supporters better than the ruler can, the ruler will quickly run out of supporters!

(This is why Russian strongman Vladimir Putin was careful to harass and imprison the oligarchs who opposed him early on in his rule. It's not just that he wanted their money; he feared that they could overthrow him, and they certainly tried.)

To prevent such calamities, the natural state needs to control commerce, as well as all other aspects of society, such as religion and education. As NWW put it, "In all natural states, economics is politics by other means: economic and political systems are closely enmeshed, along with religious, military, and educational systems."

This can even happen in democracies, and frequently does. In Mexico, for example, the PRI party had tight control over society from 1929 to 2000, dominating the national labor unions and commercial associations, extracting bribes, and distributing patronage to its supporters. Major business owners benefited from close connections to the regime, and supported PRI in return.

A slightly more benign democratic version can be found in *corporatist* or "coordinated" democracies, including several European states. Most economic activity is channeled through national business associations and national labor unions to allow for easier coordination between them and the state in setting industrial policy. Entrepreneurs who try to go it alone will often be cut off from investment capital and skilled employees; that is why such entrepreneurs often gravitate to the United States. (See *Varieties of Capitalism* in "Further Reading.")

Exercise

1. Take five minutes to list all the forms of power—loosely defined, for our purposes, as both the ability to harm people and break things, and the ability to get other people to do what you want—in your setting. Fighting ability, magical power, or command over a band of robbers count; what else?

2. Take five minutes to list all desirable goods in your setting. Money or valuables count, but so would fame, social status, immortality, attractive romantic partners, et cetera. For our purposes, let's define all of the above as "wealth."

3. For each relevant type of wealth, how might someone use different forms of power to get more wealth? List as many possibilities as you can.

4. Likewise, for each type of power, how might someone translate different forms of wealth into more power?

5. Now, imagine that centuries pass in which powerful people try to gain wealth, and wealthy people try to gain power. List at least five scenarios for how the society might end up looking.

If a given group of people became stronger over time, who else would be threatened? How might they react? Who would win? Imagine as many possible social conflicts as you can, vary the outcomes, and list them all.

6. If you are able to seize power, how is it possible to control power and wealth, and to distribute them to your supporters?

7. How can you stop rivals from gaining power or wealth?

8. If there's a sudden change—a new source of wealth, or a new type of power, or the intervention of an outside power in your society—who might benefit? Who might be harmed?

9. Of all the ideas you've listed, which have the most resonance for the story you want to tell?

The natural state is based on privileges, on favors, on connections with the ruler, on rewarding insiders with wealth taken from outsiders. It is a system ripe for conflict, where a slight change to the equilibrium of wealth and power will very likely lead to civil war.

So it's like a candy shop for fiction writers!

Once you understand the fundamental ideas of the natural state, it can fuel endless stories with endlessly high stakes. Really, the sky is the limit here.

But unless you're one of the insiders, it *really* sucks to live in one of these states.

Fortunately, not all of us do. Some of us live in societies based on rights, where someone born in poverty can become a millionaire and someone from a disfavored group can become president. It can be hard for people who don't know much about history or other countries to appreciate how incredibly rare and precious that is.

In the next chapter, we'll be looking at the *open-access social order*—the modern liberal democracy. We'll see what makes it work, but also what makes it break.

As writers, breaking things is usually more fun.

Further Reading

Peter A. Hall and David Soskice, *Varieties of Capitalism*. (This discusses the differences between "coordinated" and "liberal" market economies, many of which boil down to how easy it is to get access to investment capital without being part of the existing business elite.)

Murray N. Rothbard, *Conceived in Liberty*. (It's available for free, which is always nice, and even in an audiobook version; you needn't believe in anarcho-capitalism to benefit from Rothbard's historical discussion of early America, which mentions many details that few people ever learn in school.)

Chapter 6: Social Orders: The Open-Access State

We said in the last chapter that the natural state is based on regime control over the right to act in organizations and to carry out commerce more generally. The ruler ensures that supporters are rewarded and opponents are frozen out. If you want to get ahead in such a society, everything depends on your connections to the ruler, or one of the ruler's supporters.

The *open-access* social order is the exact opposite.

What makes it "open-access" is that *anyone* can engage in politics, form organizations, or carry out business, *without* the permission of the regime (in principle). Instead of particular insiders having *privileges*, everyone has *rights*.

To qualify as open-access takes more than just being a democracy, however. "Democracy" just means rule by the majority. You can point to many nominal democracies where the military engages in partisan politics for its own benefit or where the regime keeps outsiders off the ballot or awards economic privileges to its supporters.

(To be fair, you can find aspects of such behavior even in the classic open-access societies—Britain and the United States. But there is still a difference of degree, which matters.)

In a true open-access society, the military is no longer an instrument of political control. It has been removed from partisan politics and has become a neutral actor. Furthermore, even if some people can get cozy business contracts from the regime, or run for office with insider support, you can still run for office or start a business as an outsider.

And North, Wallis, and Weingast found that you need *both* parts: freedom of organization and political activity *and* freedom of commerce.

Why?

Each of these freedoms is profoundly fragile. It seems the way of things that as soon as people get the chance, they will try to corrupt any system to their benefit. Incumbents will always try to lock out challengers, in politics and in business. In the normal course of events, politicians and powerful businesses will do corrupt favors for each other, eventually leading to full-scale oligarchy and the rebirth of the natural state.

But it turns out the each of the two freedoms ends up reinforcing the other one.

Free political competition protects economic dynamism—because to win power in a democracy, you need to have policies that appeal to a majority of the electorate, not just a handful of rich supporters (see Chapter 15, in which we discuss *selectorate theory*). While corruption and economic favoritism are certainly possible in an open-access democracy, it is more limited in scope than in the natural state and harder to sustain.

And economic dynamism protects free political competition—because when a company is growing powerful enough to form corrupt relationships with politicians, new companies are already challenging its market dominance. With enough turnover in the economy, no single company will get the chance to buy off enough politicians before it is displaced.

For example, in 1980s America, the rise of the new computer companies disrupted the corrupt relationships between old incumbents and the political class. (See David P. Goldman in "Further Reading.")

Free politics and a free, dynamic economy. You need both, or neither lasts on its own. NWW calls this the "double balance."

Now, many readers are probably protesting right now: "That's such an idealized picture of democracy! What about the military-industrial complex, and political machines, and fake news, and…"

You're right. And that's why the natural state is the most common form of state in our history, and why the open-access society is so rare.

NWW discuss how the open-access state first emerged in premodern Britain, and it was hardly inevitable. Many unlikely things had to happen one after another—and the most unlikely of all was when the existing aristocracy began the slow process of extending their particular *privileges* into general *rights*.

And even an established open-access society is *always* in danger of backsliding into a natural state.

Bad news for citizens. Good news for writers! Remember, we thrive on conflict.

So how can such backsliding happen? There are two main avenues, which can occur at the same time:

1. The government becomes powerful enough to throttle free economic competition, making possible the longer-term incestuous relationships between incumbent companies and corrupt politicians.

2. Particular companies or individuals (or particular classes of same) become too wealthy and influential, compared to their business competitors—and compared to government officials as well. These officials will gravitate to such magnates, currying favor by selling their services.

In either case, the result is the same: political figures use their control over the economy to stay in power and enrich themselves, and their wealthy supporters use their access to power in order to stay in control of their industries. Challengers, in both politics and business, are shut out.

Ultimately, we are right back in the natural state.

And this outcome is possible even if the society remains democratic, and even if many civil rights are protected.

Nobel-Prize-winning economist Mancur Olson discusses this in his works (see "Further Reading"). He noted that it is always easier for a small group of powerful actors to lobby government for some privilege or subsidy than it is for the mass of citizens to oppose them.

If a telecom company wants to get a ten million dollar subsidy, for example, each voter might end up paying an extra ten cents. It's hardly worth it to a voter to pay attention and start a political fight over ten cents; but it's *very* worth it to the telecom company to fight for the extra ten million dollars.

This is the *collective-action problem.*

Now imagine that it's not just a single telecom company, but also agribusiness, sugar growers, auto companies, retailers, Facebook...

Over time, Olson warns, the ease with which privileges and subsidies can accumulate will result in the steady calcification of the economy and society. Interest groups of all kinds will come together to feast on the wealth of the citizenry, through direct and indirect means.

And in his book *The Rise and Decline of Nations*, Olson gives examples of entire civilizations that imploded under the weight of such privileges. The only way to prevent this outcome, Olson suggests mordantly, is for an invading army to conquer society and sweep away the whole morass of corrupt bargains in one fell swoop.

Fortunately, such an invasion can be metaphorical. Remember the double balance: free electoral competition can disrupt corrupt relationships. So can the emergence of new companies that break the stranglehold of incumbents.

But it's not easy. And success is not guaranteed.

Exercise

1. In your setting, how does political competition work? What about commercial competition? Are they kept separate, or does one influence the other?

2. Suppose you ran the government in your setting. What powers do you have to provide benefits or privileges to your supporters?

3. Which of these might a powerful or wealthy person want?

4. How can such a person reward you?

5. How could you abuse your power to extort favors from such wealthy people?

6. What if you didn't run the entire government, but you were a minor bureaucratic functionary? What favors might you give? What problems could you cause? What favors could you receive, or extort?

7. Imagine that this process goes on for a few hundred years. What could the outcome look like? Spend at least ten minutes thinking of three pathways for your society.

8. How would an average citizen be affected by such an accumulation of privileges?

9. What avenues are there in politics to fight for change? How would a "change politician" gain power and keep it? What temptations would such a politician face?

10. What avenues are there in business to challenge the incumbents? What if you broke the law in doing so? (There's a long and proud tradition in fiction of black-market commerce, smuggling, and skullduggery of all kinds!)

11. Which of these ideas have resonance for the story you want to tell?

These, then, are the real-world ways in which power and wealth are reconciled to each other:

■ Broad egalitarianism

■ The intertwining of wealth and power

■ Decoupled political and economic systems, each keeping the other in check through the double balance

Can you imagine any others? Might a different system work because of the details of your setting, such as magic? Maybe so.

Remember, though, that stories are built on conflict. When you design your system, you also have to think about how to break it.

Breaking things is usually more fun to read about.

So far, we've managed to go through six whole chapters without discussing government structure in any detail. Isn't this book called *Governments for Worldbuilders*? What gives?

Never fear. Starting with the next chapter, we'll give you a powerful model for how governments are structured that you can apply to any sort of setting you want. And we'll begin with the fundamental bases of rule: the Tripod of Power.

Further Reading

David P. Goldman, "How to Meet the Strategic Challenge Posed by China." (It's a short essay; take a few minutes to read it. For our purposes, focus on his discussion of the rise of the tech companies in the 1980s.)

Jane Jacobs, *Cities and the Wealth of Nations*. (This is a short, fantastic description of what is necessary for a dynamic economy, and why standard neoclassical economics completely misses the boat; lots of fodder for fiction writers!)

Mancur Olson, *The Rise and Decline of Nations*. (Usefully, it begins with a summary of *The Logic of Collective Action*, for which Olson won the Nobel Prize. You could also read that book in its entirety if you wish, but you'll get the gist here.)

Joseph A. Tainter, *The Collapse of Complex Societies*. (He covers a lot of the same conceptual ground that Olson does, but from an ecological point of view rather than an economic one. Tainter also provides many more cases, such as the Mayan and Chaco civilizations.)

Chapter 7: The Tripod of Power: Legitimacy

Where does a regime's power come from? In general, we can talk about three sources:

- *military* strength (typically, the army and police);

- *administrative* machinery (often, the bureaucracy); and

- the ruler's *legitimacy* with those who obey the regime.

We're going to call these factors the **Tripod of Power**. Each of these plays different roles, and each tends to weaken in the absence of the others.

In this chapter, we start with legitimacy.

Why?

Because without *some* kind of legitimacy, the other two legs of the Tripod don't work very well at all.

Why should soldiers fight for you, and possibly die? Why should tax collectors give you the money, instead of taking it for themselves? Why should subjects obey your laws, instead of breaking them for fun and profit?

A regime that can't answer those questions is going to be in deep, deep trouble.

Legitimacy is the sense that for whatever reason, a ruler's commands *ought* to be followed, and that the ruler is justified in giving them.

Even though this is the "fuzziest" leg of the tripod, it is probably the most important. Most rulers, even those dependent on overwhelming violence and threats for their continued rule, don't have enough violent capacity to threaten *everyone* at all times.

At the very least, there needs to be a reason for a ruler's top general to obey, rather than to decide that *she* should be the emperor instead! (And of course, there needs to be a reason for the general's troops to obey *her*... And so on.)

It may seem strange to think of Adolph Hitler as possessing legitimacy—and we in liberal societies tend to think he was not a legitimate ruler, since he ruled through murder and oppression. But there are more kinds of legitimacy than moral legitimacy, especially when we are talking about politics.

In a classic example, the eminent sociologist and political psychologist Max Weber identified three types: *charismatic* legitimacy, *traditional*, and *legal/bureaucratic*.

As Weber explains it, *charismatic* legitimacy is the personal magnetism of a ruler himself. If you are overthrowing the established order and claiming the right to rule in its place by sheer force of will, says Weber, you claim charismatic authority. Others who follow you will do so because of your personal virtues or power.

It is this type of authority that is typically claimed by the founder of a state, or movement, or religion. Spartacus, Muhammad, or Joan of Arc would be described as charismatic leaders by Weber, most likely. Their stature did not come from an existing political or religious establishment or formal rules; they were self-made leaders.

Traditional legitimacy is what happens when the initial charismatic leader dies. An heir is chosen, who rules based on bloodline continuity, discipleship, or some other form of connection with the original heroic leader. The original charismatic iconoclasm of the new movement becomes codified into laws and customs. In time, rulers are chosen and obeyed because that is what has always been done—tradition demands it.

A ruler's legitimacy is thus based on his conformity to the controlling tradition, illogical or superstitious though it may be. The heavy hand of history lies across such rulers, holding them in place. Opposing such a leader would be sacrilegious, a breach of the society's traditional mores. Throughout society, power and privilege tends to come by inheritance, as in feudal systems.

Legal/bureaucratic legitimacy, for Weber, is what happens when the progress of reason leads traditions to be exchanged for formal law. (Living in the *early* 20th Century, Weber was an enthusiastic believer in the transcendent power of reason.) People don't obey the *person* of a ruler; they obey the *office*.

A ruler is thus legitimate because his powers derive from legal codes and institutional procedures, such as democratic election. He is obeyed because the laws that empower him are seen as worth following. Rulers and officials also make a sharp separation between their personal lives and fortunes and their public duties.

These pure types almost never occur unmixed—most monarchies base their legitimacy on a combination of charisma and tradition, and "institutional charisma," such as that of organized churches, is usually a mixture of charisma and law.

Aside from that, there are other kinds of legitimacy, like what we saw with the big men of foraging bands— they are legitimate because they see to the welfare of their band. Your fictional society might grant leadership because of wisdom, or great strength, or whatever you wish.

However, we can still use Weber's categories as a useful shorthand.

Different kinds of rulers depend on different kinds of legitimacy, by their nature. Autocrats such as kings or dictators usually rely on charismatic or traditional legitimacy. Legalistic legitimacy is contradictory to almost all forms of dictatorship, which relies on the arbitrary use of unrestrained power.

A democracy, on the other hand, is *primarily* based on law. There needs to be a mechanism to translate the many individual voices of the citizenry into a single policy, as we'll discuss in Chapter 13. Without a broadly accepted law, a democracy is on its way to mob rule, oligarchy, or worse.

Of course, law can also have a charisma of its own. Many Americans venerate the U.S. Constitution as something like a religious text—it is the defender of our political and civil freedoms against the efforts of many political leaders to take them away.

And law can also have the weight of tradition behind it. Philosophers trying to explain why we *ought to* follow the law will often lean heavily on law's function as a coordinating mechanism for society. (For example, should we drive on the left side of the road, or the right?) Law can form a *Schelling point* (named after Thomas Schelling, see "Further Reading") that allows us to coexist more predictably. In that sense, a law can have a degree of moral force for *no other reason* than that we have had it for a long time, and people expect other people to follow it.

A ruler's source of legitimacy will be an important constraint on his or her behavior. A charismatic rebel chieftain will be more easily excused if he suddenly has his political opponents rounded up and executed than would a democratically elected president.

Conversely, the president would be forgiven for not getting a political agenda past a hostile Congress, since those are the rules of the game, whereas a queen who allows disloyal ministers to stymie her political agenda would be seen as weak.

Whatever the source of a ruler's legitimacy, the ruler had better work hard to maintain it. Once legitimacy is lost, a regime is not necessarily doomed right away; however, people will start calculating whether it is in their interests to play along with the regime, or to break whatever rules they can get away with for personal gain (see Margaret Levi, in "Further Reading"). Regime decay proceeds rapidly at this point, sometimes ending in total collapse.

Exercise

1. Thinking about your setting's ruler, what claim justifies the ruler's legitimacy? Why do the ruler's followers obey? (Examples: Is the ruler thought to be a god? Or anointed by God? Is the ruler part of a special bloodline? Or the victor in a ritual combat over the succession? Does the ruler have the most stock shares in the corporation? Is the ruler simply the richest or most powerful figure?)

2. Are there some claims to legitimacy that simply would not be accepted by the populace? (Example: rule by divine right in modern America.)

3. Does the specific form of legitimacy claimed by the ruler imply certain restraints on her behavior? Must the ruler spend time propitiating the ancestral spirits, or delivering shareholder reports, or meditating and generating magical power, or campaigning for votes?

4. If the ruler loses legitimacy, who are the very first people to start disobeying? Do they simply engage in a little private corruption, or do they actually switch allegiance to a more legitimate rival?

5. Are there competing claims for a different sort of legitimacy (for example, arguments for democratic self-government in an absolute monarchy)? Are they gaining or losing support? Why? How?

6. If so, could the existing ruler justify his rule under the other type of legitimacy? What would he have to do to stay in power?

7. Are there rivals who have a better claim to legitimacy? How?

Further Reading

Thomas C. Schelling, *The Strategy of Conflict*. (He was a pioneer in the use of game theory to analyze conflict and social coordination.)

Margaret Levi, *Of Rule and Revenue*. (This is a fantastic discussion of the bureaucratic machinery of taxation. Incredibly important is Levi's concept of *quasi-voluntary compliance*, that coercion and legitimacy interact with each other; each makes the other far more effective than it would be alone. People typically want to obey legitimate governments, and if they are tempted to hide taxable money anyway, the threat of punishment quickly convinces them to resist the temptation.)

Max Weber, "Politics as a Vocation." (This is a lecture he delivered in 1919 which is widely available online. In it, he discusses many critical topics including political legitimacy and the origin of bureaucracy.)

Chapter 8: The Tripod of Power: Administration

Just as the ruler cannot fight wars by herself, and needs an army to impose her will, the ruler also needs administrators to help manage the realm. Even in the earliest polities, with a petty king ruling a small domain out of his palace, the king would be surrounded by trusted servants who would carry out his will (see Max Weber in "Further Reading"). These would report to the ruler in his *cabinet*, or private room or closet. (From this we get the term "cabinet," or circle of high officials and servants.)

In more formalized states and as the centuries passed, these servants developed into a much more elaborate, organized structure of higher and lower officials, most of them working in a specific field run out of a dedicated office, or *bureau*—from which we get the term "bureaucrat," those who exert rule from their bureaus.

(And if you're wondering which early-modern European monarchy first elevated bureaucracy to a high art, the French terms are a dead giveaway.)

It is important to keep the origin of bureaucracies in mind. The modern reader will find it far too easy to assume that all bureaucrats in all places were like the ones we see today in the developed West—highly regimented, bound by rules, exercising impartial guidelines with limited scope for autonomy. Yet, over the course of history, bureaucracies took a variety of forms and organizational structures.

Especially in settings where communications were slow and gathering data was difficult, bureaucrats were often given a great deal of discretion in their duties. The common thread that unites all these forms under the heading of bureaucracy is that they were centralized, subject to the ruler's direction, and dependent on him for their power.

The bureaucracy has three key roles:

- transmit information to the ruler,

- execute the ruler's commands and laws, and

- collect taxes.

In each of these roles, obedience and loyalty are critical for the ruler's effectiveness; there are many opportunities for political intrigue and influence, and a disloyal bureaucrat can do tremendous damage.

(Be warned; this chapter is long and dense! But little details of a bureaucracy can be exceptionally important, and great for strengthening your setting and story conflicts. Think of this chapter as less a manual, than a menu.)

Information

Transmitting information is incredibly dependent on the individuals doing the transmitting. Think of the daily briefings that the president of the United States has on the most important matters at hand—someone needed to sift through the millions of data points, the hundreds of news events that transpired the day before, and decide what merits the attention of the president. Someone had to present the information, choosing what aspects to emphasize and what aspects to play down, or to ignore entirely (or perhaps, to conceal!).

The Assyrian empire, one of the earliest to exist, was obsessed with collecting information; of the royal documents that archaeologists have found, a surprising number of them were demands by the Assyrian king to his governors, telling them to report any event or rumor to the king, no matter how trivial.

Without reliable flows of information, the ruler is disconnected from the events of his state, unable to govern the realm in any meaningful sense. (This is true of any state, but is especially important in autocracies where power is concentrated in the ruler; the ruler needs information, more than she could possibly collect on her own.) Hence the need for trusted bureaucrats to spread their networks throughout society, penetrating as deeply as the state can manage.

Trust is the key here. Bureaucrats can choose to withhold information from the center, or even to transmit false information for the purposes of some intrigue or other. And such intrigues are common throughout history, particularly in old or dysfunctional states. In the Palace (see Chapters 10 and 11), the bureaucracy was a common player in political struggles.

Best of all would be if some powerful minister could seize the role of gatekeeper to the ruler, ensuring that all information has to go through him first, to be curated or censored at his whim. (Depending on the setting, a strong queen might play a similar gatekeeper role for her husband, and so could a favored concubine in palaces that featured harems.)

As a result, rulers had to keep a close eye on their servants, sometimes by setting up shadow institutions staffed by trusted confidants to check the work of official bureaucracies. Often, the trusted inner circle would be made up of agents of lesser station than the nobles and grandees who make up the "official" government organs. These men would be elevated by the ruler for their achievements, and were totally dependent on him for their position.

In recent times, autocrats tend to have several different intelligence services, each of which keeps tabs on the others; an early example was noted by Hannah Arendt in her study of Nazi Germany and the Soviet Union (see "Further Reading").

Exercise

1. In your setting, how does the ruler keep tabs on her kingdom and neighbors? How much can she observe directly, and how much has to come from intermediaries?

2. Who are the intermediaries? Are they trustworthy? Do they compete with each other?

3. Are there any mechanisms to ensure their loyalty?

4. What schemes are afoot to mislead the ruler? To what end? How might they be discovered?

5. What information is handled by lesser officials, so as not to bother the ruler? At what point are problems big enough that the ruler has to be told?

Executing the Laws

Bureaucrats are tasked with carrying out the ruler's will—often by collecting taxes (see next section), but not exclusively. Rulers might regulate commercial practices, modes of dress and behavior, religious observance, and many, many other aspects of daily life. If these regulations are to have any teeth, they must be executed by the bureaucracy.

Generally, this means that the bureaucrats need security forces, like the military or police, to provide the muscle. Bureaucrats might serve as judges or investigators, or that role might fall to the local mayor or governor. (In feudal Europe, the local lord often judged crimes and disputes that fell under his jurisdiction.) In any case, for a law to be enforced, there need to be people doing the enforcing.

The bureaucracy's reach does not always extend far into society. In developed countries today, a powerful state administration deeply penetrates into citizens' daily lives; but this situation only dates back maybe a hundred or two hundred years. Historically, most state bureaucracies were small and could not extend very far into society before they ran up against their limits—perhaps down to the city level, or even the province level.

At the point where the bureaucracy's reach ended, the administrator would have to interface with the local power-holders—who we will call *notables*.

Notables

Notables could take many forms, depending on the society. They could be rich or powerful, like petty noblemen or gentry. They could be held in high esteem by the local populace due to their scholarship, such as the Confucians in China or the rabbis or *ulema* of Judaism and Islam respectively. They could be representatives of a religious organization, as was the local bishop in Europe. They could be part of a village council of elders, or traditional tribal leaders.

But whatever qualifications they had, the notables had the support of the populace of their regions. State officials needed their cooperation to get anything done; in many cases, the notables would mediate between the state and their society, receiving the state's demands for taxes or troop levies, and then using their own position to see that these demands were met (or not!). For example, in many societies the state would assess taxes on a town or village as a whole; town officials would then be free to collect the taxes from individuals as they saw fit.

Most imperial governors have to be careful when dealing with the locals, or they will soon find themselves impotent. This is especially the case when the governor speaks a different language than the people of his province; he would be totally dependent on local translators or "fixers" to get anything done. In large empires with slow travel times, it was common for provincial governors to become more sensitive to the interests of their local notables than to the distant emperor—and in some cases, to even "go native."

Bribery

Often, bureaucrats demand side payment from their hapless customers before doing their jobs—issuing a business permit, say, or approving a new house. Just as often, bribes are offered by people seeking to evade the laws.

It is important to understand the difference between the two. Bribes to break the law are a malfunction of the system. But in many cases, when an official refuses to do his job until the client pays, that is the system.

In much of the world, officials are chronically underpaid by the government, and are tacitly or openly expected to make up the difference from the populace. (In the Ottoman Empire, for example, the pervasive system of hierarchical bribery was dignified with the term baksheesh.)

Even modern humanitarian groups who loudly deny paying bribes to corrupt officials will sometimes make a distinction in practice, when they are in the field. They will define a "bribe" as "paying officials to do what they should not do." But "paying officials to do what they should already be doing" is called a "facilitation fee"!

Whether or not the distinction matters morally, you can make use of the difference in your worldbuilding.

Exercise

1. Who enforces the ruler's laws, or commands? Are there different enforcers for different kinds of law?

2. How large are these organizations? How far do they extend throughout society?

3. Do they depend on the cooperation of local notables? How cooperative are the notables? How much influence do the notables have on the officials?

4. Are the enforcers corrupt? Are they bribed? By whom?

Taxation

Regimes run on money. Sometimes, they can get that money from regime-controlled resources, like oil wells, or salt mines dug out by slaves. Sometimes the regime may monopolize lucrative commercial industries like long-range trading expeditions. Most of the time, the regime's money comes from the populace through some kind of taxation.

In America, we are used to income taxes being automatically deducted from our paychecks, which then get reported to the IRS. But if you think about it, there's an awful lot of infrastructure that goes into making something like that possible (see Margaret Levi in "Further Reading"). And for most of history, that kind of direct proportional taxation was simply impossible.

Instead, most governments relied on methods that didn't need as much information about how much money an individual had, such as:

- fixed fees, such as head taxes, poll taxes, or permit fees;

- taxes charged at geographical choke points, like customs duties at a port or border crossing; and

- tax farming.

(What is tax farming, you ask? I'm so glad you did! In the general category of bureaucratic methods, tax farming is one of my favorite topics. Yes, I'm a nerd. See below.)

Needless to say, the choice of what to tax, who to tax, and how harshly is going to have dramatic effects in your setting. Whether you choose to oppress the peasants, to squeeze the greedy bankers, or to exact levies from your surly nobles, the details of taxation are a fertile ground for story conflict.

This is particularly true for tax farming.

Tax Farming

In its basic form, the ruler created some sort of tax or tariff—a ten percent tax on salt, for example—but rather than collecting the taxes himself, the ruler would sell off the right to collect the tax to some private party. This was the *tax farmer*. The tax farmer would pay a large sum up front to the government, and in exchange would gain the right to ruthlessly apply the salt tax to anyone within his jurisdiction and pocket the proceeds.

This allows a ruler without an existing tax administration to get revenue upfront, often several years' worth of revenue at once. But it comes with significant drawbacks.

First, the tax farmer, and not the state, is the direct beneficiary of tax revenue. Let's say a tax farmer paid 1,000 gold crowns for the right to collect the ten percent salt tax for the next five years, and then proceeded to collect 3,400 gold crowns. All that money goes to *his* pocket, not the state's. Furthermore, the tax farmer is *only* interested in his revenue; he doesn't need to worry about the welfare of the peasants, or their willingness to serve in the army during wartime. That gives the tax farmer a tremendous incentive to sacrifice long-term social welfare for short-term gain.

In general, tax farming was often incredibly lucrative for the farmer, while the state was forced to sell the future revenues at discount prices, simply because it lacked the capacity to collect taxes itself.

The French monarchy, for one, was heavily dependent on tax farming for revenue. This dependence was a major contributor to the French Revolution, for two reasons. First, royal revenues were always rather stunted because the tax farmers absorbed much of the take, weakening state power. Second, the tax farmers of France were notorious for harshly oppressing the populace in order to squeeze every last *sou* that they could. Similar concerns were at play with the Publicans of ancient Rome. (See "Further Reading.")

Tax farming can also appear in more subtle forms, especially in modern society. Take casinos, for example. They pay a large sum of money to local and state governments, and in return gain the right to siphon vast amounts of money from willing gamblers. The voluntary nature of the transaction makes it more palatable, of course, but even then the addictive nature of gambling muddles things.

Even more striking is the history of the banking system. That subject is so fascinating that it deserves its own chapter, but for now, suffice it to say that in the early 1800s, many U.S. states raised nearly half of their revenue by selling monopoly banking charters. A particular bank would pay large sums in exchange for exclusive control of its town, free to earn considerable profits from its residents. In the 1880s, president-for-life Porfirio Díaz managed to do this with the national bank of Mexico!

The idea of tax farming is a useful lens for viewing much government policy. Other examples can be seen, or invented, with only a little effort.

The key thing to remember is that a ruler turns to tax farming when she needs more money that she can easily extract with her own servants. It is the hallmark of lands with difficult travel, poor communication, and weak and divided political loyalties. In time, the tax farmers can become extremely powerful in their own right, perhaps even rivaling the established authority.

Exercise

1. How does the government in your setting collect taxes?

2. What kinds of things are taxed? Land? Agricultural products? Trade goods? Fancy houses?

3. How much information does the state need to collect taxes? How does it get that information?

4. Does the state collect revenue via private tax farmers or close equivalents?

5. Which social classes are taxed more than others? Which social classes or smaller groups of people benefit from the tax system?

6. What tensions or conflicts are being caused by the tax system?

You can see how bureaucrats have a tremendous amount of practical power. As the bureaucracy goes, so goes the regime.

And that makes the question of *trust* critical. Even today, with video monitoring and spyware on work computers and everything else, it's easy for a rogue bureaucrat to cause a lot of trouble. In earlier times when it was harder to monitor behavior, having the wrong bureaucrats was crippling.

In the worst case, the bureaucracy could effectively take power for itself. This often happens when the nominal ruler is ineffective—either because he is personally incompetent or dissolute, and leaves the details of rule to his advisors, or because the bureaucracy has become powerful enough that only a gifted ruler can actually seize the initiative from them. In either case, the ruler becomes a figurehead—but is still the locus of legitimacy for the regime.

The Mandarinate of Imperial China is perhaps the classic example of this; often, the Chinese emperor had little true power and spent most of his energies on ritual activities and pleasure-seeking, while the byzantine departments of the Mandarin bureaucracy actually ran things.

If rulers wanted to avoid such ignominy, they *needed* ways to keep their officials trustworthy. Often, this was done by ruthlessly punishing lawbreaking. Creative governments could also design social systems that promoted trustworthy behavior in their bureaucrats.

A good example of such a bureaucracy was the English aristocracy, between about 1600 and 1900 (which includes the Jane Austen and "Regency" genres; see Douglas Allen in "Further Reading"). Unlike in earlier eras, where the nobility derived most of its income from its lands, during this period a noble's lands were usually *unprofitable*—by design. Aristocrats were expected to take large tracts of their land out of production and turn them into public walks. They were also expected to build massive, expensive homes which were open to visiting aristocrats at all times, and these homes were not merely away from the cities but even away from the local village.

Moreover, noblemen were expected to go to the right schools. Less obvious was that these schools were remarkable in deliberately avoiding "practical" learning. Nobility were taught Latin, Greek, literature, and a whole host of topics which were utterly useless at making money. Furthermore, if a would-be aristocrat had made enough money to buy land and aspire to the nobility, he was expected to *immediately* stop practicing his profession. For an aristocrat to engage in business was considered terribly shameful.

Why were aristocrats hobbled in these and many other ways? To turn them into utterly loyal servants of the king. The important thing to know is that most nobles made nearly all of their money from salaries, by serving as royal officials—which could earn them ten times as much as the most successful businessman, at the time. They served at the king's pleasure, and could be dismissed for any reason. As a result, the kings of England had access to a class of loyal servants—of uncertain ability at times, true, but whose dedication was nearly unquestioned. And it was this class of nobles that won England and Britain its empire.

Further Reading

Douglas Allen. 2009. "A Theory of the Pre-Modern British Aristocracy." *Explorations in Economic History*, Vol. 46: 299-313. (Allen lays out his theory that the strangest practices of the English aristocracy were designed to transform the aristocrats into the perfect servants of the king.)

Hannah Arendt, *The Origins of Totalitarianism*. (This is a deep study of how Nazism and Soviet Communism arose, and how the regimes stayed in power. It is sobering reading, but has lots of good details for worldbuilders.)

United Nations of Roma Victoria, "Roman Taxes." https://www.unrv.com/economy/roman-taxes.php. (This has a brief but nice discussion of tax farming in early Rome, the problems that it caused, but also the benefits it provided.)

Margaret Levi, *Of Rule and Revenue*. (We mentioned this last chapter, but it's worth repeating. Levi takes a deep dive into how taxation systems were first built, and what constraints they needed to work under. Highly recommended!)

Noel Maurer and Andrei Gomberg. 2004. "When the State is Untrustworthy: Public Finance and Private Banking in Porfirian Mexico." *Journal of Economic History*, Vol. 64, No. 4: 1087-1107. (How does a government that never pays its debts manage to borrow money anyway? First, create a national bank...)

Max Weber, "Politics as a Vocation." (See specifically his discussion of the development of bureaucracies.)

Eugene White. 2004. "From Privatized to Government-Administered Tax Collection: Tax Farming in Eighteenth-Century France." *Economic History Review*, Vol. 57, No. 4: 636-663. (Available free from SSRN.)

James Q. Wilson, *Bureaucracy*. (This is the classic work on American bureaucracy, which goes beyond simplistic criticisms or praise and asks *when* the bureaucracy works, *when* it doesn't, and what makes the difference. Exceedingly useful.)

Chapter 9: The Tripod of Power: The Military

Mao Zedong said that political power flows from the barrel of a gun. He *also* said (and this is less remembered) that, therefore, the Party must control the gun, and the gun must not control the Party.

In other words, the brute facts of violence are important, but so are the social arrangements that control them.

Whoever has *control* of violence will tend to gain political power. This is as close to an iron rule of history as you can get.

In several times and places, the military did not actually rule society, but submitted (for the most part) to a legitimate authority. The United States is a decent example of this, as are most of the European powers in the last few decades. But more frequently, those with the means of violence make the rules.

That said, it makes a *huge* difference what the state of military technology is, for that will determine if weapons are available to the mass of people, or if they are restricted to only an elite few.

Samuel Finer argued in his monumental *The History of Government from the Earliest Times* (see next chapter) that when weapons were widely available, politics tended to feature mass participation and broad egalitarianism, if not outright democracy.

The classic case is the ancient Greek city-states, particularly Athens. Military tactics of the time relied on mass armies made up of pikemen called *hoplites*. These hoplites generally provided their own weapons and armor, so they had to be prosperous enough to afford them. However, the level of training needed was relatively low by modern standards, so cities could field large armies— and needed to! Thus, they *also* needed the loyalty of a large segment of their populace.

It is no coincidence that in Athens the right to vote extended only to men who could afford to serve as a hoplite.

Similarly, many have argued that the early American experiment in democracy was underwritten by the mass ownership of muskets and rifles, which would end up being crucial in the American Revolution against England and in dissuading tyranny afterwards.

On the other hand, when expensive weapons give special advantages to those wealthy enough to afford them, power tends to be concentrated in the hands of a few.

For example, the rise of powerful kings in Europe had much to do with the advent of cannon—fantastically expensive to make, requiring a large specialized infrastructure of foundries. In particular, with cannon the French kings were able to reduce the fortresses of their rebellious nobles, consolidating their own power.

In an earlier age, the armored knight was the undisputed master of the battleground, able to crush unarmored opponents with ease. Thus, power tended to be held by the armored warlords of the feudal era, whose rule depended on their use of naked force.

Then the free Swiss militias developed their famous style of pike warfare, which nearly nullified the advantages of the knight.

Max Weber argued that the rise of the Israelite kings over a previously egalitarian society was the result of advanced armor, which gave a significant battlefield advantage to those wealthy enough to buy such armor.

Changing weapons technology can also help explain the modern rise of child soldiers. P.W. Singer (see "Further Reading") argues that child soldiers are now more common because small arms are becoming more advanced and lighter. Young children can now use weapons effectively on the battlefield in spite of their small size and physical weakness, which had not been true for most of human history.

As a result, child soldiers are becoming a frequent sight in war-torn areas, since it is relatively easy for a brutal warlord to coerce children into fighting.

Similar issues are beginning to arise because of drone technology. Robots have often been used for fun by hobbyists; but they are now increasingly weaponized, and made available off the shelf. Governments will likely be unable to stop the spread of drone weapons into the general populace, and the social effects of this shift are likely to be extreme.

A great fictional example of such social shifts is given in the webcomic *Schlock Mercenary*, by Howard Tayler. Early on in the series, the resident mad scientist develops long-range teleportation (the "teraport"), removing the need for interstellar travel through warp gates as had been the norm. This threatens the power of the Gate Guardians, triggering a war; but it *also* allows people to teleport bombs directly into their enemies' homes, setting off a rash of violence across the galaxy that only ends once scientists figure out how to create teraport-denial fields.

If your setting contains magic, the same principles apply. How common is magic? How destructive?

If magic is common, then most people will have access to some kind of magic. The popular militia may be powerful enough to challenge a central ruler, since its magical prowess could outweigh the advantages of a professional army.

If magic is rare and requires a long apprenticeship, perhaps the ruler has managed to centralize all magical training under his control, and all mages are required to serve in the army. Or perhaps mages are viewed as dangerous dissidents, training in secret with their masters and periodically emerging as the shock troops of yet another rebellion.

Or perhaps a new style of magic will disrupt the existing status quo, leading to a glorious golden age or a terrible civil war.

Exercise

1. In your setting, how common are weapons (or magical abilities)? How expensive are they?

2. Are they easy to learn and use, or do they require specialized training?

3. Do "commoners" have a martial tradition, or is soldiering restricted to a professional class?

4. Do powerful or wealthy people gain military advantages from their wealth? Are the most effective weapons and armor also the most expensive? By how much?

5. Would a mass army of commoners be able to defeat a specialized professional army?

6. Does the overall balance of military power favor a warrior class or caste, professional armies backed by the wealthy elites, or the common militia?

7. How does this feed into politics? Is the political structure in tune with military realities? If not, what pressures are building up, and how will they be resolved?

8. Could a new weapons technology upset the balance of power? What changes would it cause? Who would gain the most from it?

Why is a strong military or security service important to state power?

For Samuel Finer, the answer is clear: the core of a state's power is its ability to extract resources from the populace. Without taxes or plunder, the state simply has no resources to work with.

And historically speaking, the most fundamental means that a state has to extract resources has been its military. With a strong military, the state is not only able to defend its own borders from invasion—a crucially important task—but it can also force its subjects to pay taxes, and it can plunder neighboring lands.

With the additional revenue, the state can build out a more capable tax-collection bureaucracy (see previous chapter) and invest even more in its military, which in turn allows it to press its claims more harshly and extract even more, and so on.

Now, militaries and police forces are not *only* about taxation and plunder. In a dangerous world, you need to be able to defend against invasion, or you just get conquered and sometimes slaughtered to the last man, woman, and child. And to have an army, you need to be able to pay for it *somehow*.

Regardless, Finer notes, "Throughout the history of government, warfare, and hence the expenditure on the armed forces, has [usually] been… the single most extravagant and continuous drain upon the fiscal and economic resources of the state."

(Of his case studies, the only exceptions were early Egypt and Mesopotamia, which instead spent much of their resources on gathering and redistributing food.)

On the other hand, spending less on the military is *not* usually a sign of benevolence by the state; it is instead a sign of weakness. In much of Africa, for example, states often cannot protect their own borders or resist invasion or uprising; and many military units operate as semi-autonomous bandits, supporting their operations by plundering the populace with the blessing of the state itself. In Congo, the expression went, *civil azali bilanga ya militaire*—"the civilian is the cornfield of the military."

Army Composition and Loyalty to the Regime

But the military and police force presents a major problem to a ruler—any force powerful enough to resist invasion, maintain civil order, and collect taxes is *also* powerful enough to overthrow you and seize power!

And history is full of ambitious generals who did just that.

So what is a ruler to do? There are many ways to keep the troops loyal, such as ideological indoctrination, high pay, or other forms of social control. But for now let's focus on army composition.

By "army composition," I don't mean how much infantry you have versus cavalry, or battle mages versus dragons, or whatever—though that is clearly important. And if you do like to think about that kind of thing, questions of unit type can easily fit into the model we are about to discuss. But a ruler fundamentally must build his military from three kinds of troops:

- popular militias,

- a professional national army, and/or

- foreign mercenaries.

The popular militia is the cheapest and easiest option, if your objective is to defend against invasion (or, sometimes, to do a spot of invading yourself). Responsible for their own training and equipment, militiamen do not represent a drain on the treasury as other types of soldiers do, and they can be raised quickly when needed. However, they tend to be relatively poorly trained and armed, and are therefore less effective in battle than a standing army.

But militiamen are loyal to their families foremost, their nation second, and the regime a distant third—if at all! Especially if you plan on being a squeeze-the-peasants sort of ruler, allowing the people to organize into armed units would be the last thing on your mind.

A standing army remedies many of the defects of the militia. Soldiers are better equipped and better trained, dependent on the regime for their pay, and also more easily indoctrinated politically (if that kind of thing is a feature of your regime). However, professionalized armies take a long time to train up, and are fantastically expensive.

Moreover, while soldiers in a standing army may be more loyal to the regime than your average peasant is, they will still care more about the nation as a whole—and might decide that the ruler needs to go for the public good. Alternatively, one of your commanders may decide that he wants your job, and convince his men to back him. A standing army thus represents a permanent threat to the regime, more urgently than the populace as a whole does.

The Roman legions demonstrated this danger time and time again; when they felt it necessary, they would cheerfully depose one emperor and replace him with another.

A less-expensive compromise is for regimes to employ foreign mercenaries, who come already trained. On the other hand, the loyalty of mercenaries is notoriously fickle, and they can betray their employer whenever convenient. In *The Prince*, Machiavelli provides a whole host of examples where Italian city-states were abandoned and even conquered by the mercenary bands of *condottieri* they hired.

Net-net, as Finer writes, "Rulers have to make a choice—or arrive at a combination—of three priorities: efficiency in battle, expense, and loyalty. Different kinds of armed forces correspond to each of these priorities."

So what to do?

A common pattern in history was for a regime to have a large, cheap popular militia, and a smaller standing army as shock troops in battle—and also to garrison the imperial capital, to keep the rural militias from getting uppity! Meanwhile, the ruler would have a personal bodyguard of foreign mercenaries: dependent on him alone for their pay, generally resented by the populace, with fewer links to any scheming local rivals, and in danger of being massacred by the army if the ruler ever died.

Of course, a wealthy regime that was not loathed by its people could have the luxury of a powerful full-time army; the United States is one example today. But even the U.S. still maintains a distinction between the Army and the National Guard, which could be seen as a rough parallel to the popular militias discussed above. A better example would be the Iraqi army under Saddam Hussein; the bulk of the military was poorly equipped and paid, while the smaller Republican Guard—recruited exclusively from Hussein's own clan—was a relatively elite force whose performance, and loyalty, were more assured.

In many countries, strong militaries are often a greater threat to their own regimes than to the enemy. This is certainly true in Africa, South America, and much of Southeast Asia. As a result, regimes often deliberately starve their militaries of resources—to the extent that they can safely do so. (Such militaries are often *very* good at demanding larger budgets at gunpoint.) However, this makes the military less effective on the battlefield; during a real war, regimes often have to employ Western mercenaries—paying high prices—to have any hope of victory.

Exercise

1. What external threats does the regime in your setting face?

2. What internal threats does the regime face?

3. How easy is it to collect taxes? Would having more troops or police make it easier?

4. Are the people loyal to the regime? Does the regime trust them with weapons? Are militia effective enough on the battlefield to make them worthwhile?

5. Can the regime afford a standing army? Will they stay loyal?

6. Can the regime afford foreign mercenaries? Are there particular skills or capabilities that foreign specialists would add, like a rare kind of magic or alchemy, or photonic-drive space cruisers?

7. What mix of militia, standing army, and mercenaries provides the best political mix for the regime's needs?

8. What happens if the regime chooses poorly?

9. What happens if the regime loses legitimacy? Which military units will mutiny first?

10. Are there any ambitious generals or groups of colonels thinking about a coup?

11. Which of the ideas you generated has resonance for your story?

Further Reading

S.E. Finer, *The History of Government from the Earliest Times*. (This is a massive, massive three-volume work of history and political analysis that is without equal.)

Maiah Jaskoski. 2013. "Private Financing of the Military: A Local Political Economy Approach." *Studies in Comparative International Development*, Vol. 48, No. 2: 172-195. (Available for free download at https://core.ac.uk/download/pdf/36737239.pdf. Jaskoski looks at many cases in which formal military units in weak countries actually hire themselves out for pay, sometimes with the tacit encouragement of the government. Fascinating stuff.)

Niccolo Machiavelli, *The Prince*. (If you want to know politics, you have to read Machiavelli. 'Nuff said.)

P.W. Singer, *Children at War*. (This is a sobering, analytical look at child soldiers and their growing use. If your story features any child soldiers, this book should be required reading.)

Howard Tayler, *Schlock Mercenary, Book 1: Tub of Happiness*, particularly the arc titled "Battle for the Wormgate"; and *Book 2: The Teraport Wars*. (Just don't start reading when you have something important to do... for the next week or so...)

Chapter 10: Introduction to Polities

We've discussed the nature of politics. We've looked at some dynamics of class conflict, and how wealth and power have a fraught relationship with each other. We've gone over the Tripod of Power: legitimacy, military, administration.

Now that we've established the foundation, we're ready to dive into the fun stuff:

Who's the boss?

Societies are big and complex. You could have farmers, merchants, nobles, religious figures, all jockeying for position in your politics. If you're trying to create a fictional setting, keeping track of it all can be overwhelming. And figuring out what political setups make sense, *and* how they create compelling story conflicts, can be too much to handle.

Which is why so many authors default to your typical "kings and princesses" fantasy setting. All the work is done and you don't have to think about it much.

But you want more. You want to write something meaty, something fresh.

Wouldn't it be nice if you had some kind of clear, simplifying *tool* to help keep everything straight!

That way you could have a broad structure for your society, which will guide you as you invent all the cool little details and keep you from getting lost in the weeds.

In the rest of the book we are going to be discussing two powerful models from political science that can *also* be very useful tools for writers who want to do effective worldbuilding. These are the *polities* model of Samuel Finer, and the *selectorate theory* of Bruce Bueno de Mesquita and his collaborators.

The polities model tells you who rules society. Selectorate theory tells you how they stay in power, and when they lose it.

Pretty important to know, right?

For the next several chapters, we'll discuss the different components of the polities model.

Samuel Finer was one of the greatest political scientists of the United Kingdom in the Twentieth Century. His crowning achievement was a three-volume work, *The History of Government from the Earliest Times*, which is exactly what it sounds like. He surveys governments from ancient Egypt to modern Europe, analyzing what made them work and fail.

It's a stupendous work. And after being out of print for years (I had to scour used-booksellers for my copies!), it's finally available again.

The details about each society are great for worldbuilding and even for general historical interest. But you don't have to read all thousand-plus pages to use the polities model, because we're about to give you the key bits.

Finer gave us an invaluable way to look at governments. In his model, a government could be ruled by four kinds of actors, alone or in combination:

- **The Palace**—this is a centralized regime from which power and authority flows; the king, or emperor, or dictator.

- **The Nobles**—these are powerful figures who are *autonomous* from the Palace.

- **The Clergy**—their power and influence derive primarily from religious or ideological sources.

- **The Forum**—this is the enfranchised part of the people, who collectively engage in politics on their own behalf.

We'll call each of these a *Regime Actor*. The specific pattern in which a society is ruled is called a *polity*.

For example, you could have a Palace polity, a Forum polity, or combinations such as Palace/Nobles, Palace/Clergy, Forum/Clergy, *et cetera*.

So for us worldbuilders, in designing our setting we have a fundamental question to answer: *which of the four ruling groups is in power, and how do they relate to each other?*

Let's take a closer look at the Regime Actors.

The Palace

This is the central locus of power; the core of the regime. It is usually headed up by a single, immensely powerful ruler. The Palace is the main concentration of political, bureaucratic, and military capability in the state. The ruler of the Palace is usually (but not always) the single most powerful being in the country; and in many settings she is an absolute ruler, without any legal restraints on her power.

That does *not* mean that the Palace ruler can do whatever he wants, however. Depending on your setting, he may be faced by a recalcitrant bureaucracy, dangerous relatives, legal or constitutional restraints, or the open opposition of some of the other three Regime Actors.

And in a few rare cases, the social system is so decentralized that no true Palace exists.

The Nobles

What makes the Nobles distinctive is not that they are powerful or influential. In any polity there will be influential figures, even in the Palace. Indeed, it is common for a class of aristocrats to be attached to a Palace and make up its bureaucracy, as we saw in Chapter 8. But in

Finer's model, such figures are called *courtiers*, because their power depends on their participation in the Palace court.

For a group of powerful people to be considered Nobles in the sense Finer means, they must have *autonomy* from the central government, and from each other. The Nobles are able to *resist* the central government, because they control their own power resources—land most frequently, but also the people on that land.

In more futuristic settings, "Nobles" might be powerful corporations with unique technology that the government relies on, so that they cannot risk antagonizing the Nobles. Or they could be the local governments of planetary colonies, effectively out of reach of the distant central government since space travel is so slow.

One might think that a vast fortune would be an autonomous power resource as well, and sometimes it can be. But rich people sometimes become hostages to their wealth, which can be threatened by a powerful central government. Often, a regime is able to force wealthy actors into a subordinate role, within a *corporatist* system.

Corporatism

Corporatism **does** not **mean "rule by corporations," except in the duller internet chatrooms. It actually refers to an ideology advocating the organization of individuals into** corporate actors **such as national labor unions, national business federations,** scientific guilds, et cetera, so that each group of people can better advocate for its interests and direct its behavior—or, less optimistically, each regimented group of people can be better controlled than could unruly individuals. This can be compatible with democracy, as in the Scandinavian countries (see "Further Reading"), but is also a hallmark of Fascism, in which all the corporate bodies are under the control of the central government. As Benito Mussolini put it, "All within the state, nothing outside the state, nothing against the state."

Nobility is hardly a black-and-white affair; you can imagine a sliding scale of "nobleness," ranging from being entirely autonomous from the Palace, to being all-but-dominated by it. Very few Nobles can actually *ignore* the Palace entirely. And some Noble classes are in a precarious position, with the Palace growing increasingly strong and threatening Noble power.

But, often, Nobles are able to preserve their own privileges and power in the face of the Palace, and even to threaten the Palace itself. (This makes the Nobles the natural enemy of courtiers, who see their own advancement tied up with the fortunes of the Palace.)

A class of Nobles is a great feature for generating story conflict!

The Clergy

The power of the Clergy derives from its claim to represent some transcendent Truth or Power: the divine, or historical law, or occult wisdom. People obey not (primarily) from coercion, but because they *believe* in what the Clergy represents or its special expertise.

Clergy in this sense could take many forms. The most common historically have been religious clergy like the Catholic Church, of course; but in a fictional setting you could have a class of state-sponsored "scientific" experts, ideological propagandists, philosopher-kings, or whatever you like.

Usually, Clergy do not rule on their own; but when supporting another Regime Actor, they can provide a powerful boost to a regime's legitimacy. Think of the role of German university professors in supporting Nazi Germany, for example.

The Forum

Earlier, we noted egalitarian societies in which no true state exists, and where people of the society share a voice in the major decisions of that society. In the Forum, the rule of the people is explicit and formalized. State institutions exist to carry out the needs of society, but they are subject to the people and depend on it for their orders. Formal mechanisms such as voting, written law and public law courts, and public debate translate the opinions of individuals into a collective imperative that is sovereign over the government administrators.

Forums can take several forms—and they need not include *everyone* in the population. In ancient Greek democracy, for example, the vote was restricted to free males who were heads of their households, and often who met certain criteria of wealth. Most of the time, fewer than ten percent of the residents of ancient Athens were eligible to vote. But such a limited voter pool is still broad enough to go beyond a narrow aristocracy or oligarchy, broad enough to include significant parts of the people itself in its self-rule.

A Forum need not be a democracy either. It could be based on deliberative councils of tribal elders, such as the councils of ancient Israel or modern Afghanistan, in which each elder represents the interests of his clan as well as the collective interest. (Such councils may emerge even against the wishes of an autocratic regime!) It might be a techno-futuristic system of crowdfunded government budgets. The main point is that some sort of mechanism allows the people, or a large enough chunk of it, to have a voice in public policy.

Forums have many potential points of failure, which we'll discuss in greater detail. But they are a natural opposition to a Nobility, and to many kinds of Palaces. Given that most of us live in Forum polities (or to be precise, Palace/Forum polities), it's no surprise that the rule of the people frequently shows up in fictional stories as well.

In the next few chapters, we'll be looking at each of the "pure" polities, where society is ruled by a single Regime Actor (starting with the Palace polity).

We'll discuss what makes it distinctive, the role played by class conflict, what social orders lend itself to this regime, and also how the polity relates to the Tripod of Power. (This is where it all starts coming together!)

We'll also look at some *hybrid* polities, in which multiple Regime Actors share power, or fight over power—for example, the Palace/Noble polity, a common type in which a powerful king nevertheless has to deal with a nobility that is nearly as powerful and jealous of its privileges.

Further Reading

S.E. Finer, *The History of Government from the Earliest Times*. (Especially Volume I.)

Peter J. Katzenstein, *Small States in World Markets*. (This is a pathbreaking discussion of corporatism in democratic countries such as Sweden. It is probably responsible for all the politicians wishing that America were "more like Sweden," though history has been somewhat less kind to neo-corporatism since the book was written.)

Chapter 11: The Palace

Most regimes throughout history have featured one person at the top. Whether the ruler is an absolute despot, oversees a hierarchy of fractious nobles, is first among equals, or is a constitutionally restrained chief executive, power has a way of concentrating in one set of hands. This Regime Actor is called the *Palace*.

Even in a polity where the ruler of the Palace is *not* actually powerful enough to impose her will on society, and is not even the *most* powerful component in the regime, structurally speaking the Palace has many advantages in the long term. We'll discuss those soon; for now, however, let's start with the case in which the rule of the Palace is totally unchallenged: the *Palace polity*.

In a Palace polity, all politics are focused on a single person: the ruler, who has ultimate and arbitrary power.

The ruler could be called king, empress, dictator, president, or any number of possible titles. She may preside over an aristocracy or other sorts of important people, or an official political party like the Nazi or Communist parties. He might be a war chief of a marauding tribe, or the chief stockholder of a megacorporation. But what distinguishes the pure Palace polity is this:

All subjects, including the aristocrats and other notables, are totally dependent on the ruler—they do not have autonomous power, and their privileges depend entirely on carrying out his or her will.

If the ruler wishes, he can grant land and titles to a loyal retainer, or take them away from someone in disfavor. In many ancient societies (such as the old Canaanite city-states), the ruler was even able to take away the wife of a subordinate, and assign her to someone else!

Within the state, the ruler's power is formally unlimited, without procedural constraints of the sort we expect in a liberal democracy. The power of all others depends entirely on their proximity to, privileges from, and influence over the ruler.

This means that under normal circumstances, the goal of political maneuvering by underlings is to gain access to the ruler, and gain her trust. Such trust becomes a prized resource, and people in gatekeeper roles (such as personal servants, spouses or concubines, or chief ministers) are often able to exploit their position to guide policy. After all, the ruler's decrees will be strongly affected by what information is able to reach her!

Ironically, even though such a Palace ruler would be incredibly powerful compared to the prime minister of a democracy, absolute rulers in the modern era have a much harder time *keeping* power. The rewards of being the sole ruler are vast, and the threat of betrayal or rebellion is incredibly high. Historical monarchs were slightly better off than modern autocrats, because they could lean on the divine right of kings or something similar to buttress their position; moderns don't generally believe in the divine right of kings, so autocrats have to work harder to justify themselves.

Which takes us to legitimacy.

Legitimacy

In a pure Palace polity, legitimacy *always* derives from some form of charisma or tradition. In other words, there is something unique about the ruler that justifies his power or else the traditions that empower him are impossible to break.

Charisma could also be "routinized" and become a form of tradition, as when the hereditary ruler claims to be a god. Rulers could claim the divine right of kings, or the Mandate of Heaven, or some other transcendent blessing justifying their rule.

A ruler might also simply be at the top of an aristocracy, with no greater justification than its existence. His rule is supported because he upholds the position of the aristocracy and advances its interests effectively.

But whatever the exact form of legitimacy, the ruler is ultimately responsible *only* to the power or beliefs grounding her rule: the gods, or God, or the harmony of the universe, or the nobles who put her there.

The ruler is not required to justify himself to *anyone* else—especially not the people. Finer states that all of the types of legitimacy claimed by a Palace polity are, "without exception, authoritarian. There is no question of popular sovereignty. The monarch's authority descends on him from a Higher Power and sets him above the people."

After all, if power *does* come from the people, then what would make the ruler special? And what would justify the ruler's arbitrary power?

Thus, the typical Palace polity is built on a fundamental claim: *ordinary people have no right to political power, or political rights.*

(But what if the ruler *did* claim to represent the people? Then we would no longer have a pure Palace polity, but a Palace/Forum polity—an incredibly important type that we'll look at in Chapter 13.)

Legitimacy is not a blank check; even rulers claiming the divine right of kings were often overthrown. But strong legitimacy will give would-be plotters pause, because it will make it harder for them to gain support. People will obey the Palace not just out of self-interest, but because the Palace is *entitled* to their obedience.

Losing Legitimacy

Still, even with an authoritarian style of legitimacy, it is possible for the ruler to behave badly and lose her legitimacy.

For example, if you claim to be a god, or to have some metaphysical relationship with the cosmos, you will be required to act the part. You might have to follow a purity regimen, or perform magical rituals every day, or bestow blessings and mercies on your worshippers.

Fail to do so, and your abused followers will soon decide that you are putting them all at risk by neglecting your divine duties. But perhaps your infant son will do better...

Similarly, if your rule is based on the Mandate of Heaven, or simply the claim that you'll do a better job of running society than the democratic government you overthrew (as in many Latin American *juntas*), you had better deliver the goods. If you're clearly competent, you might survive a few bad years as people trust you to weather the storm; but if you're a drunken sot, you might be a single famine or economic crisis away from losing power.

Basically, the legitimacy of the pure Palace regime rests on its performance—or the *perception* of performance.

Losing legitimacy by itself won't necessarily cause the ruler to be overthrown, especially if the military stays loyal; but it will make everything else harder. Every official in the bureaucracy will be chiseling a little on the side, soldiers might be less willing to die for you, tax collection will go down, and laws will be broken more frequently.

It is for this reason that modern dictators spend so much effort on enhancing their own legitimacy, especially by coopting the media. (It is worth noting how many TV personalities and journalists in the United States are married to politicians or government bureaucrats. And other regimes are much worse!)

Some even go to the point of setting up cults of personality—such as the North Korean regime, with its dubious claims that Kim Jong Il was a champion archer and athlete.

Administration

If you have a single ruler sitting in her throne room in the Palace, she will depend on trusted deputies to carry out her decrees. In an early era, these might actually be personal household servants, as we noted in Chapter 8. A more elaborate regime might have a formal bureaucracy, but this would probably be very different from the modern ideal of the bureaucrat as the impartial administrator of the law. The duties of the Palace bureaucrat are:

- transmit information from the outside world to the Palace and

- carry out the orders of the Palace.

Not to mention the ever-present addendums:

- protect your own position or secure advancement and,

- where possible, extract bribes.

(Lest we become too judgmental, even today there are many regimes in which bureaucratic graft is openly acknowledged and condoned by the regime, as we noted in

Chapter 8. Often, this is because the regime cannot afford to pay reasonable salaries, and depends on its bureaucracy to be "self-funding.")

Good information flow is critical for all governments; but for the Palace regime it is especially essential, because all authority and policy flows downward from the ruler. If the ruler is kept out of the loop, everything falls into chaos.

Practically speaking, there might be high levels of autonomy for local officials in some regimes. But in principle an imperial edict might be issued by the ruler at any time that totally sweeps away local policies in favor of a blanket rule that could be hideously inappropriate to actual conditions. The only factors to prevent such outcomes are good information and wise advice from subordinates.

When a bureaucracy becomes corrupt, or actually subverted by enemies of the Palace ruler, the ruler can rapidly become impotent. Without the right information, she wouldn't even know if her orders are being followed. Without efficient administration, she might run out of money to pay her army.

Ultimately she might be overthrown, or might be left as a mere figurehead, free to amuse herself in the royal pleasure-gardens while true power lies in the hands of others.

To defend against such undermining, many Palace rulers will set up their own parallel bureaucracies, made of hand-picked, loyal personnel. Where the official bureaucracy might be made of aristocratic "courtiers," fat and secure in their positions and difficult to discipline, the "shadow" cabinets might even be made of commoners—or in any event, people who are totally dependent on the ruler's favor. Such loyal servants can help keep the official bureaucracy in line, sometimes, and can provide more trustworthy sources of information to the ruler.

The Military

Usually, whatever ideologies support the rule of the Palace, its survival ultimately depends on its military. (And the police, if the two are distinct.) However, as we discussed, the military is also the greatest threat to the ruler!

In modern autocratic regimes, the military often becomes a powerful interest group, pressuring the government to follow policies it favors and extorting lucrative privileges. Often, the military owns major businesses and controls commercial trade, exploiting its superior logistics and organization (not to mention the threat of killing its competitors!). One could accurately compare such behavior to that of the mafia, but at a much larger scale.

And sometimes, a powerful general simply decides to seize power from the ruler.

How can a Palace ruler prevent these problems?

One effective strategy is fear. Constantly replacing one's military leadership prevents any one general from becoming too comfortable, and also from building relationships with other officers that could prove dangerous. And rigidly enforcing rules on the common soldiers tends to restrain the usual abuses of the populace.

But who can be trusted to watch the military? And then who watches the watchers?

This is usually presented as a paradox, but many regimes have found a way out: have *several* security organizations, including intelligence organizations—and use each of them to control the others. This is basically the same strategy we saw above with the shadow bureaucracy, but often has a higher body count.

For example, in the Soviet Union, there were several competing intelligence and secret-police services: the KGB, the GRU, SMERSH, NKVD, and so on. Organizations were formed and dissolved seemingly at random. While each of these services nominally had its own niche, they were also competitors with each other and with the military. The Soviet secretary-general could, if necessary, order agents from one organization to arrest officials from another.

(Fun fact: the United States has *seventeen* known organizations in the "Intelligence Community," including the prominent ones like the CIA, FBI, or NSA, but also separate intelligence services for each branch of the military, as well as for the military as a whole. The rivalry and bad blood between the CIA and the FBI is legendary.)

The ruler of a Palace polity has formally unlimited power, but also faces endless dangers. Some of these are well-trodden ground in fiction, like rebellions and poison in the wine. But some are more subtle, like an army with questionable loyalty, or a bureaucracy that hides critical information from the top. A setting that featured this kind of conflict would be interesting indeed!

Exercise

1. Thinking about your ruler, what is the source of his/her power?

2. What claim justifies the ruler's legitimacy? Why do the ruler's followers obey? (Examples: Is the ruler thought to be a god? Or anointed by God? Is the ruler part of a special bloodline? Or the victor in a ritual combat over the succession? Does the ruler have the most stock shares in the corporation? Is the ruler simply the richest or most powerful figure?)

3. Does that claim to legitimacy exclude the possibility of popular sovereignty or other forms of rule?

4. Does the specific form of legitimacy claimed by the ruler imply certain restraints on the ruler's behavior? Must the ruler spend time propitiating the ancestral spirits, or delivering shareholder reports, or meditating and generating magical power?

5. Who are the members of Palace "court"? How might their power or influence be dependent on the Palace? What

privileges do courtiers have because of their proximity to the Palace?

6. Does the ruler have any ways to control or circumvent his or her courtiers?

7. How might the Palace prevent the growth of independent powerful figures (Nobles)?

8. How can the courtiers influence the ruler?

9. If the ruler is feckless or incapacitated, which courtiers might usurp effective (but not de jure) power?

10. How might the ruler be overthrown? Is such an overthrow consistent with the existing ruling ideology, or would it need to put forward a new ideology?

11. Looking back over all the ideas you've written down, which have the most resonance for your story?

Further Reading

Niccolo Machiavelli, *The Prince*.

James C. Scott, *Seeing Like a State*. (This is a tale of bureaucracy gone bad; how in their quest to reshape society to make things easily counted, controlled, and categorized, modern states often cause tremendous harm to ecosystems they don't understand.)

Chapter 12: The Nobility

A class of Nobles is distinctive. To be a Noble in the sense we mean, you have to be at least mostly autonomous from the Palace, and also from other Nobles. In the pure case, a Noble is distinguished by his absolute control over those in his domain. No higher authority, no central government, may interfere with a Noble's lands or vassals.

In a certain sense, each Noble domain could be compared to its own miniature country. This helps to explain why nobles were constantly occupied with feuds and intrigues against each other. On the other hand, Nobility could often arrange themselves hierarchically or even fractally, so that many petty lords could be vassals of a more powerful lord, who in turn would be one of the several vassals of an even more powerful lord, all the way until you reach a handful of great nobles who dominate their politics, and who were often bitter rivals.

Much of Medieval Europe worked this way. Samuel Finer also gives the example of Muromachi- and Sengoku-era Japan, with its samurai class aligned under the *daimyo* lords, in ever-shifting coalitions and factions.

To have a pure *Nobility polity* is almost, but not quite, a contradiction in terms. It would have to lack a Palace or central government altogether, leaving the nobility to be totally in charge of its affairs. On the other hand, there still has to be some mechanism that ties the nobles together into a single country—otherwise, you wouldn't have a single regime, but a patchwork of many smaller principalities, each ruled by a small Palace.

So how do you tie together a bunch of autonomous nobles?

The only real-world example that Samuel Finer locates is that of 16th-17th-century Poland, where the great nobles sat in a council together, under the nominal rule of a king who nevertheless was totally controlled by the noble council.

Or, a Nobility might lack a formal mechanism of unity, but belong to a shared ethnicity or other identity group that is in conflict with its neighbors, forcing a sense of shared fate. The Comanche tribes, although not a Nobility, would be a good example of such informal unity; without much in the way of formal government, the Comanche managed to fight long and successful wars with neighboring tribes and with Spain, Mexico, and (for a time) the United States.

But in any event, to have a Nobility polity work, you need to know *why* it works.

Pure Nobility polities are extremely unstable. Over time, they have a tendency to either coalesce into a stronger central government, becoming a Palace/Nobility polity (see below), or to break apart entirely.

You can see this general dynamic in political unions such as the American Articles of Confederation, where the states were co-equal sovereign regimes and the Confederation government was quite weak. It risked breaking apart in open warfare, and the political class responded by creating the Constitution, which instituted a much more powerful Federal government. A similar struggle is presently raging in the European Union, and there it seems like a breakup is more likely.

The fracturing of a Nobility is particularly likely when individual nobles find it in their interest to betray their peers and the polity as a whole, by allying with foreign invaders. This was common in Renaissance Italy, where the feuding political parties in a given city-state would often ally with outsiders whenever their rivals were in power. In a real sense, Italian nobles felt little loyalty to their city— which is part of why the rise of Italian nationalism meant the destruction of the old aristocracy.

But the disintegration of a Nobility polity can take a while; unstable equilibria can still last long enough to be interesting for fictional purposes!

Palace/Nobility

We noted that a pure Nobility polity is quite rare, due to the lack of a unifying factor; more commonly, Nobles coexist uneasily with some sort of centralized Palace—perhaps a High King ruling over local kings, perhaps a formal state government that has poor control over its unruly outlying provinces. Such cases fall under the *Palace/Nobility* polity.

In general, a Palace/Nobility polity is marked by continuing tension between the two Regime Actors. The situation will differ depending on which is more powerful: the Palace, or the Nobility.

If the independent nobility is relatively weak, then while nobles have their ancient privileges, those privileges might be closely circumscribed. Palace administrative structures may be imperfect, so local control depends on the cooperation of the nobles, but the nobles will face endless competition from the courtier class, whose prestige depends on the largesse of the Palace alone.

Weaker nobles would have small armed forces if any; they pose little threat to the Palace in the long run. And unless there is a dramatic change in the balance of power, the Nobles' position will erode over time.

But if the central monarch faces a powerful set of nobles with strong militaries of their own, she must scramble to keep on top of them via careful alliances and shrewd politicking or risk losing power, or being made nearly irrelevant. Think of the early French kings, or of King John of England (who was forced to sign the Magna Carta by an alliance of barons).

This circumstance can have several long-term outcomes. In the case of England, the rights that the nobility extracted from the king (in the form of the Magna Carta) laid the groundwork for the English experiment in broad political rights, the forerunner of the more explicit American political rights that created the modern liberal-democratic society. That did not happen in France, where the nobles focused not on rights but on privileges—chiefly, the privilege of taxing the populace. As a result, even when the French monarchy grew in strength, it still had to depend on tax-farming for revenue; the resulting abuses of the people were a key factor leading to the French Revolution.

For a weak ruler to strengthen his position is a long, perhaps generational, project. It took the Capetian kings of France hundreds of years to slowly, patiently, methodically chip away at the power of the nobility, and they were never assured of ultimate success. The same could be said of the English kings, who suffered periodic overthrow and wars of succession. An effective nobility can defend its own position quite effectively; still, the king has the advantages of a central political position and the ability to divide and conquer, given the opportunity.

In short, a patient monarchy may be able to slowly accumulate power in spite of the nobles' opposition; but the nobility might just as easily keep the monarchy stunted and under its control. We'll just have to read your story to find out…

Legitimacy

This will vary with the type of Nobility we are dealing with. If it is a blue-blooded aristocracy, then it might rely on a doctrine stating that the Nobles are intrinsically higher than commoners, and entitled to rule by right of birth. (This might be part of a full-blown caste system.) Such a doctrine might entail some reciprocal sense of *noblesse oblige*, duty to the common folk; or it might not.

(It's worth noting that an ideological division of society between nobles, freeholder peasants, serfs, and slaves is *incredibly* common throughout human history, and is often mirrored in a society's religious beliefs and cosmology. Initial differences in wealth and power tend to be justified after the fact as simply the way things *ought* to be.)

If the Nobles are wealthy magnates, on the other hand, particular nobles might gain good reputations as patrons and good stewards of society; but their legitimacy as a class will rest on the fundamental legitimacy of the economic system they prosper under. If a noble's wealth is not seen as her due, then the oppressed common folk will try to take it from her, when they can.

If the Nobles are merely jumped-up bandits with their own armies, legitimacy as such will be hard to come by. Even then, however, smart warlords will go out of their way to act as patrons and benefit the local community, and gain its loyalty as a result.

A good real-life example was Jérôme Kakwavu, commander of the *Forces Armées du Peuple Congolais*, a mercenary band that dominated part of northeastern Congo from 2003-2005. Jérôme's forces were brutal outside of areas he controlled, but within "his" territory he charged low taxes to attract economic activity, donated money to the local university and football team, and distributed thousands of T-shirts with his face on them to residents. Jérôme was much preferred by the locals to the corrupt national government, for all of his brutality and lack of formal legitimacy.

Administration

To some degree, each of the Nobles functions as a miniature Palace within his domain. So the same issues we discussed in the previous chapter would apply here, in theory. In practice, Noble domains are often much smaller than your typical Palace-regime state; as a result, administration might be less formalized, less structured, and more reliant on delegation to local notables.

So administration might be carried out by trusted personal servants, in the mode of an early royal household as we mentioned. The noble herself might take a more active hand in the process as well, since her domain might be smaller and more manageable.

In early-modern Poland and Russia, nobles often lacked the administrative skills necessary to run their estates. Instead, they resorted to a type of tax-farming called *arenda*, in which operator-investors called *arendators* would lease major assets from the noble, such as mills, taverns, or distilleries, or the right to collect taxes and customs as in conventional tax-farming. The noble got a steady income, plus he could offload the headache of administering his lands to the arendators. As an added bonus, the peasants hated the arendators more than the noble who empowered them! (This was one of the factors leading to Khmelnytzky's Rebellion in 1648, which featured terrible massacres.)

Of course, depending on your setting a Noble might rule over a vast domain that would compare to some Earth empires (or some Earths!), and could thus preside over a fully professionalized bureaucracy.

At the same time, the Noble's regime has to coexist uneasily with that of the central authority, whatever that looks like. Sometimes the Noble's retainers will be free to run the domain as they wish; sometimes they will have to work around restrictions from the central authority.

Military

Similar issues are at play here. If the noble has a large domain, his military might be as formalized and professional as with any Palace. But if the domain is small, the noble might not be able to sustain a large professional army and would have to depend more on militia levies, or on mercenaries if he can afford them.

If the professional army corps is small enough, the noble might fight at their head, and the soldiers might know her personally and feel personally loyal. This might alleviate some of the problems that a Palace would have with a military that evolves into an interest-group. It might also get the noble killed…

Crucially, the strategic problems of an individual noble are somewhat different from those faced by the regime as a whole. Defense of the realm is one thing, but even more important is defense of the noble's own domain—not least from other nobles! This might lead to a situation where (for example) the nobles' collective armies are optimized for low-level skirmishing against each other, and become poorly suited to repelling a major threat from the outside.

Exercise

1. Spend five minutes thinking about your Nobility. What makes the nobles independent of a central authority like a king? What is the source of their power? Do they have land? Their own militaries? Control over trade routes? Magic?

2. What feature of this region, or your larger setting, makes it difficult for a central authority to project power and control the nobles? If there is no such feature, why hasn't a king or other powerful ruler arisen yet? Is it simply too early in history? Or was there a ruler before, who became weak or was overthrown?

3. Is there a nominal central ruler, like a high king or president? Is the ruler weak and getting stronger, weak and getting weaker, strong and getting weaker, or strong and getting stronger?

4. How might the nobles take power from each other over time? How might the nobles take power from the central ruler? How might the central ruler take power from the nobles?

5.   Does the central ruler have a "courtier" class? How are courtiers rivals to the nobles?

6.   Are the nobles organized in any sort of council? Do they have bonds of loyalty or partnership or citizenship? What ties them to each other? (If no such ties exist, then they are not strictly speaking "nobles," but a collection of autocrats ruling over many tiny states.)

7.   What rivalries exist between different nobles? How might someone else exploit them?

8.   Which of the foregoing answers resonate with the story you want to tell?

Chapter 13: The Forum

Palace rulers or aristocratic nobles can be powerful; but they still make up a tiny fraction of the populace. Often, even in oppressive settings, the people are able to build systems to express their political demands. They could be town-hall meetings, assemblies of respected elders, formalized voting systems, or something else entirely. But the key is that the dispersed individuals of a population are transformed into political units that are able to make demands or set policy. This is the *Forum*.

If the Forum actually rules society, having displaced a Palace or Nobles (or if it never had them), then you have a *Forum polity*. This could take many forms, and might exclude some parts of the populace. For example, perhaps only landowners have the right to vote, or to participate in open debate.

Or, political decisions might be made on a town-by-town basis, with little national coordination (as with the Hanseatic League).

Forums need not have the "standard" concept of citizenship, which was an invention of Greek democracy.

In Greek city-states, the city was a sort of corporation in which the citizens had equal shares, and thus an equal say in governing. Hellenistic citizenship did not necessarily include the concept of civil rights, which was arguably invented by ancient Israel; likewise, the Israelite Forum was composed of assemblies of elders, rather than democratic voting.

Nor would Forums necessarily be egalitarian. Perhaps they are dominated by a rising merchant class, while the farmer class is too busy gathering the harvest to show up at the assembly. Perhaps city-dwellers have more influence than those in the country, for the same reason.

Aristotle famously described Athens as having a "mixed" government, where some offices were popularly elected, some chosen by random lottery, and some held by powerful magnates. (We would probably call that a Forum/Nobility polity.)

Regardless, the Forum is the mechanism by which the people rule themselves.

But remember Chapter 6, and how we saw that the *open-access* social order can be easily corrupted back into the *natural state*. Similarly, Forums can very easily lose their power to autocrats or oligarchs over time.

Still, the process is not set in stone.

And in any event, it provides us writers with many fabulous opportunities for political conflict.

Forum/Nobility

The Forum/Nobility polity was less common historically than some of the other types we have discussed, because democracies of any kind were rare until recently, and modern democracies would not tolerate the kind of unequal division of power that Forum/Nobility implies. Still, there were some. For a polity to be classed as Forum/Nobility, says Finer, the general body of voters would have to grant special powers to a much smaller class of nobles. The most familiar example is probably early-Modern England, which featured the House of Lords and the House of Commons.

Similar systems were in place in some of the cities of the Hanseatic League. Going back earlier in time, the late Roman Republic offers a fascinating example, in that the whole society was striated by civic tribe—the more powerful tribes voted first in the Centuriate Assembly, and if their vote was unanimous the other tribes would not vote at all.

Finer writes that the Forum/Nobility configuration cannot last. The balance between the Forum and the Nobility is unstable; there is no "natural" division of power between the two groups. Each side will try to erode the powers of the other over decades or centuries, and usually the nobility wins. In the end, the polity is reduced to a pure Nobility or oligarchy. On the other hand, in the modern U.K. the House of Lords has lost nearly all of its former power, and has been eclipsed by the House of Commons.

Legitimacy

We noted that the Palace and Nobility polities typically rested on ideologies that emphasized the superiority of the ruler over the ruled. In the Forum, it is the opposite. Several variants of Forum ideologies could be present, but the common thread is that the people as a whole have a right to self-govern.

This doesn't necessarily mean that all people are *equal*. Remember that democratic Athens withheld the vote from slaves, women, and the poor. In that case, voting rights were given to those who served in the military, and only them. Early America likewise restricted the vote to property-owning men.

Still, in general, the idea that the populace ought to hold power is an attractive one, as we know today. Once a Forum ideal is established in a society, it can be incredibly tenacious and hard to displace. Certainly, ideas of divine right of kings or inherently superior aristocracies have a hard time reestablishing themselves—their basic premises are usually exploded by the idea of the Forum.

(If you have a setting in which some people are *literally* superior—possessing magical talents, or actual descendants of the gods, or members of a more intelligent or stronger species—all bets are off.)

Yet democracies do perish, and are often replaced by oligarchies or dictatorships. Why?

There seem to be three major routes for the Forum to lose power, and degenerate into a Palace/Forum regime:

1. Power gradually accumulates in the hands of the executive (see below in "Administration.") The representative or popular structures of the Forum give up more and more practical authority, until at last the executive controls everything. In a democracy, you might see (at least initially) a situation where voters freely elect a powerful ruler, called a *plebiscitary dictatorship*.

2. Society becomes increasingly stratified. Wealth and power, and especially military power, becomes concentrated in a few hands. The ability of the people to participate in the Forum becomes attenuated, and eventually the oligarchs simply sweep away or subvert the Forum regime.

3. The Forum regime becomes ossified, or split by factions, or the people themselves lose their unity and sense of shared fate. The upshot is that the regime is unable to quickly respond to crises, no matter how urgent. In such a situation, a strongman is likely to emerge to forcefully deal with the crisis, the Forum be damned. Such strongmen tend to stick around after the crisis is over. The rise of Benito Mussolini over a dysfunctional Italian republic is the example of excellence here, and worth serious study. (Often, legitimate Forum executives such as presidents can step into this role.)

Palace/Forum

Napoleon, Hitler, and Stalin all ruled from a supremely powerful Palace. Yet we said before that the pure Palace regime claims legitimacy due to its inherent superiority over the people it rules. *These* tyrants had a much different ideology—they claimed the right to rule *as representatives of the people themselves*. In this way, they still nodded to the legitimating ideology of Forum rule.

This is the mark of the *Palace/Forum polity*: a powerful central government that still claims legitimacy as representatives of the popular will.

In principle, the autocrat is simply a trustee of the people, rather than its master. In practice, this might even be true; the modern United States is effectively a Palace/Forum that, even though imperfect, is far better at actual representation (for now) than were other Palace/Forums such as Nazi Germany, the Soviet Union, or any one of a dozen *caudillo* rulers in South America. But as these examples make clear, even nominally democratic Palace/Forums need not remain so for long, if too much power accretes in the hands of the Palace.

The powers of the ruler in a truly tyrannical Palace/Forum polity are absolute or nearly absolute. The people have no real involvement in their rule; their role instead is to serve as either passive observers of the ruler who claims to act on their behalf—as in most military dictatorships—or as active shock troops of the regime, obeying the orders of the Party and magnifying its power without actually exercising power themselves—as with most totalitarian regimes such as the Fascist, Communist, or National Socialist varieties.

Still, as long as the Palace keeps claiming legitimacy as a trustee of the Forum, its behavior will be markedly different from a pure Palace regime. (But not necessarily *better*.)

Now, it is possible for a relatively *weak* Palace to coexist with a Forum; the difference will hinge, perhaps, on two factors:

- the level of centralization found in the administrative apparatus, and

- the level of autonomy from popular oversight that the administration has.

But whatever criterion you apply, the key is that the voice of the Forum is still decisive. Popular institutions still work, laws are respected, justice is widespread, and popular sovereignty is still exercised over a constrained executive to a considerable (if not perfect) degree.

Administration

In a Forum, there needs to be some structure to translate people's individual views into public policy. Once this is done, you also need structures to carry out that policy.

In some settings, these structures are one and the same. The early parliaments, for example, were able to insist on a role in royal government specifically because (and *only* because) they directly controlled tax collection. The "power of the purse" was not merely procedural, but actual. (See Michael Herb, in "Further Reading.")

You might also imagine a situation where particular representatives oversee law enforcement, or commercial regulation, or whatever.

Another common pattern is for the Forum structure to empower executives, or even entire bureaucracies, who derive their authority from the people but are free from day-to-day control. This is typical in modern democracies, simply because our parliaments don't want to be bothered by the details of running fantastically complex societies.

The danger here is that the actual power of the executive might grow, to the point that executives and the bureaucracy become independent of the Forum's control. That way lies oligarchy or dictatorship, as we saw above.

In the United States, we mitigate the risk (slightly) by directly electing our executive (the President). In many parliamentary systems, the Prime Minister is appointed from the elected parliament itself.

Still, the *Principal-Agent* problem of who controls the bureaucracy remains a key vulnerability of the Forum.

Military

Usually, a Forum was made up of a nation in arms. Remember that one of Finer's main arguments is that political power tends to correspond to the distribution of military force. One of the most important factors underwriting the continued power of the Forum, even in hybrid regimes, is that the regime depends on the loyalty of the people to survive—and is willing to trade political participation and rights to secure that loyalty.

In early pre-state societies, nearly all able-bodied men (and occasionally women) were considered warriors. Weapons tended to be simple and were widely available, so that the distribution of power between people was fairly even. This is one of the factors sustaining an egalitarian social structure, as we discussed before.

Even as societies grow more complex, Forum polities usually continue to have mass involvement in the military. The Athenian phalanx and the Swiss militias are key examples. The United States was founded by the American colonists' rebellion against the British, made possible by their widespread ownership of firearms. The French Revolution was sustained by the *levée en masse*, a new style of warfare in Europe in which large numbers of poorly trained citizens fought against Austro-Prussian professional armies that were much smaller.

Changing technology often brings with it a change in the distribution of military power, and soon political power as well. Ancient Israel is a good example, as Max Weber argues. In the early days of the pre-monarchy tribal confederation, the Israelites served in popular militias, largely on foot and without heavy armor. (Thus, in the Biblical account of Deborah's war against the Canaanite general Sisera, the Canaanites possess heavy chariots which the Israelites could not match. They therefore forced battle in the hill country, where the light infantry of the Israelite militia could negate the Canaanites' advantage.)

The power of the popular militia restrained the growth of centralized political structures in Israel, for a time. Later, the arrival of heavy armor, chariots, cavalry, and foreign mercenaries increased the military power of those wealthy enough to afford them, creating the basis for a ruling class; the first monarchy emerged shortly after.

In modern settings, some argue that the American idea of a popular militia restraining the power of a central government is a fantasy, in light of nuclear weapons, centralized surveillance, heavy bombs, and the like. Others rebut with the examples of Afghanistan and Iraq, in which even such overwhelming technological advantages did not automatically secure victory for the more powerful side.

Exercise

1. What gives the people real power against a would-be ruler or oligarch? Is it military weaponry? Broad wealth? Magic?

2. What institution translates people's individual wishes into a unified policy? Is it an elected legislature? A popular debate followed by a vote? Discussion and consensus by tribal elders? A shared religious law that dictates behavior?

3. Who has the right to participate in the above institutions, or to choose representatives? In other words, who is enfranchised? (Remember that the famed Athenian

democracy, for example, included only about ten percent of the city's males.)

4. Are decisions made effectively, especially in crisis moments? Is the process too slow? Does it have a tendency toward alarmism? Can voters be bought off or intimidated?

5. Are there groups of people who are specifically excluded, like slaves or women, or elves, or biological humans in a cybernetic society?

6. If the populace makes a decision, who carries it out? In other words, who is the executive or executor? Are they selected, or elected, or hereditary, or something else?

7. How might the executive actor gain power over time? How might it gain power suddenly? How might it lose power, and/or legitimacy?

8. What changes in society might undermine the basis for the Forum polity? List at least five.

9. What ideology justifies the Forum, instead of a monarchy or other non-participatory form of government? How might that ideology be challenged? Does the ideology threaten any neighbors?

10. Looking back at your potential points of conflict, which have the most resonance for your story?

Further Reading

Michael Herb. 2003. "Taxation and Representation." *Studies in Comparative International Development*, Vol. 38, No. 3: 3-31. (He discusses the way in which early parliaments directly controlled taxation, forcing kings to pay attention to them.)

Hendrik Spruyt, *The Sovereign State and Its Competitors*. (For those unsatisfied with Tilly below, Spruyt discusses several more complex cases. In particular, he asks why the same kinds of political conflicts in Europe resulted in dissimilar governments, such as centralized royal states, weak nobility-dominated kingdoms, and the decentralized Hanseatic League. Lots of good detail, if you can wade through the opening chapter.)

Charles Tilly, *Coercion, Capital, and European States, AD 990-1992*. (This is a corrective to Finer's emphasis on coercive taxation. Tilly notes that, often, the wealthiest states were those that provided political rights to their taxpayers in exchange for cooperation. He also talks about the different patterns of historical development between states based on rights and states based on coercion.)

Chapter 14: The Clergy

Many political problems can be overcome with excessive violence. Rulers tend to be an amoral lot, disregarding decency and justice in the pursuit of power. But even the most hardened warlord, even the mightiest empress, is sometimes brought up short by religion—and by its bearers. These are the *Clergy*.

The Clergy need not be pacifists, and might have armies of their own. They might even be the rulers of their own landed domains, as many bishops in Medieval Europe were. But what makes Clergy distinct from the merely pious is that they demand obedience based on their religious stature, which in turn comes from their own subordination to a religious standard.

The Catholic Church is an obvious example. So would be the leadership of the Church of the Latter-Day Saints, or Martin Luther and his circle. Their power depended on the cooperation of their followers, who believed that obedience to the Clergy was obedience to the divine.

There were times in Medieval Europe when the pope was able to raise up kings and cast them down, and when

the Catholic Church had the most powerful bureaucracy
and intelligence systems around. (This was largely because
few Christians outside of the Church could read.) But while
sometimes the Church could call on military forces of its
own, typically its power depended on its moral authority—
the widespread belief that the Church's dictates *ought* to
be followed, even by nobles or monarchs. No surprise
that even today, clerics are often the only figures able to
publicly resist powerful tyrants.

Maintaining that moral authority usually requires that
the Clergy act and make sacrifices in accordance with its
religious teachings, and demand such sacrifices from the
populace and other rulers—at least in public!

A pure Clergy polity is vanishingly rare—Finer
identifies only the Vatican and the historical Tibetan
theocracy as pure Clergy polities. (Perhaps he could
have added modern-day revolutionary Iran, which is at
the very least a Clergy/Forum polity.) Far more often, a
Clergy is subordinate to another Regime Actor and gives
it legitimacy; the most common of these is Palace/Clergy.
This is perhaps because the Clergy's own legitimacy
depends solely on religious justifications, and usually
excludes a justification based on political or military
power. (Indeed, a Clergy that actually justifies itself
based on its coercive power is probably in the middle of
a collapse of its authority.) Instead, endorsement by the
Clergy turns obedience to the Palace into a religious virtue.

A Nobility/Clergy polity would be unusual, since
a fragmented nobility would coexist uneasily with a

centralized Clergy; but Finer does note one example, the Teutonic Order during its bloody rule of East Prussia and the Baltic, starting in the 1200s: "The Order consisted of three classes of brethren: the priests, the serjeants, and the knights. These knights had to be both noble and of German blood. There is no mistaking the religious nature of the Order; no brother might hold private property or marry, and all had to follow a very harsh discipline and rule."

For Clergy to rule along with the Forum would be difficult, since rule by God often exists in tension with rule by the people. Finer suggests one exception: Congregationalism, when the people choose their own religious/political leaders, almost always in small communities where people know their neighbors face to face.

I would add another possibility: when the Clergy sees its role as maintaining a religious ethos that underpins effective rule by the people, such as a taboo against monarchs or military dictatorship. The prophets of ancient Israel may have played this role, with their frequent criticisms of the ruling class.

Conversely, as in Iran, the theocracy could hold veto power over the Forum elements. For example, it could be that only pious politicians would be allowed to serve in the parliament, as judged by the Clerics.

Non-Religious Clergies

Up to now, we've been assuming that the Clergy we are talking about is religious. But really, you can imagine many organized bodies who claim that people should obey them because they, and only they, represent the truth.

University professors and scientists sometimes claim special expertise on policy—often far outside of their own domains of scholarship. (Noam Chomsky, for example, is a trained linguist yet often holds forth on political matters.) Perhaps a government of technocrats might feature in your story, setting policy on scientific grounds only instead of bowing to sordid politics (or so they would tell themselves!).

Perhaps the study of philosophy is viewed with reverence, as in Confucian China, so that the pronouncements of philosophers become tremendously powerful.

Perhaps the ruling regime is based on an official ideology, and has a cadre of political commissars embedded in with the security services and bureaucracies—nominally outside of the normal chain of command, but able to ruin careers and destroy lives with a word.

Perhaps a cohesive media establishment shares a worldview that is different from that of the populace it broadcasts to, and media figures work patiently to change minds by the millions.

In any case where a powerful or influential group does not appeal to raw force, or to existing laws, but to moral, intellectual, or ideological arguments, you can make the case for a potential Clergy as we discuss it here. You just need to tweak the religious language a bit, and it will still work.

Legitimacy

Religious legitimacy may be the very strongest form that exists, when done right. It can combine the weight of tradition with the dazzling awe of charisma, all backed up by the threat of divine punishments for disobedience.

The catch is that the Clergy needs to avoid hypocrisy. As long as clerics obey their own rules, demonstrating their own submission to the divine, a religious populace will believe in their rectitude; but if clerics become corrupt, exploiting their position for material gain or flouting their religious doctrines, the people will quite reasonably ask why the Clergy merits obedience in the first place.

This process can take a while. In Europe, the Catholic Church was arguably corrupt and decadent for centuries before the Protestant Reformation, and many of the people retained their own piety all the while. But eventually, something has to give. Either there will be a reform movement within the Clergy itself, or a competing religious leadership will arise from the lay populace, or an alternative religion (or lack of same) will challenge the Clergy for dominance.

Religious competition can also happen in the absence of Clergy corruption. A competing faith may arrive from distant lands; a new philosophy may be developed that challenges the gods. Heresies may break out among the people—such heresies often justify violence against hated elites, or encourage otherwise-forbidden physical pleasures, and thus risk becoming quite popular.

In any event, as religious beliefs fracture, the Clergy loses power. Part of its charisma is the sense that obedience should be automatic. Once this is gone, even moral stature can only go so far. Today's pope might call for a president or prime minister to resign, but no one will listen.

(On the other hand, under John Paul II, the Catholic Church was critical in the fight against oppressive regimes in South America and Eastern Europe; but it was a *long* fight, and difficult.)

Administration

This will vary widely by the type of Clergy. However, one important factor is that *if* the Clergy and its administrators are sincere in their beliefs, they will be far more effective than most. There will be less need to monitor administrators for disloyalty or corruption, more leeway for individual initiative, and less use of coercion to enforce its rules on the populace. (Note that "less" need not equal "zero.")

Also, by their nature Clergy tend to be better educated (in particular subjects) than the average. In some settings, this might give them a significant advantage—for example, if only Clergy know how to read, or if only they can speak the Ancient Language of Power.

As such, Clergy often make up an important part of the bureaucracy of regimes even where they are not in charge. This is especially so if they control the education of the young.

The Military

Similar to Clerical administration, a religious military can take many forms. But again, if soldiers' religious beliefs are sincere, they can become fearless in battle—especially if the Clergy promises them supernatural benefits such as Paradise, salvation, or divine protection.

(In your setting, this might make them more effective, or it might make them less—for example, as with the suicidal *banzai* charges of despairing Japanese troops in World War II.)

Clerical influence can be more subtle. One of the factors allowing the Catholic Church to influence military behavior in Christian Europe was papal rulings on the property rights of soldiers to their plunder. In wars considered "just," soldiers had much stronger rights to carry off plunder legitimately than in wars that the Church did not sanction. As a result, warring sides had at least some incentive to fight just wars, as defined by the Church, or their soldiers would lose property rights to their plunder.

Exercise

1. What religious/spiritual beliefs does the Clergy have in your society? How do those beliefs justify its political power?

2. Is the Clergy the sole ruler? Does it exercise veto power over another Regime Actor? Or does it provide legitimacy for another Regime Actor, like a king with divine right? What kind of legitimacy?

3.   Does the Clergy make political demands on other powerful figures, or society in general? How are these enforced? Does the Clergy have an army, or magical power? Or do people obey because of its moral authority?

4.   What sacrifices must the Clergy make to demonstrate its religious piety? What sacrifices does it demand of others?

5.   Does the Clergy observe its own rules? Does it have the respect of the people? Of the elites?

6.   How can members of the Clergy exploit their positions for personal gain? How often do they do so?

7.   What happens if a member of the Clergy has a crisis of faith? What about someone not in the Clergy?

8.   What would happen in a religious schism? Or a sudden outbreak of unbelief?

9.   Looking over all the potential conflict points you've noted, which have the most resonance for your story?

We've now covered each of the four Regime Actors in the Polities model of Samuel Finer: the Palace, the Nobles, the Forum, and the Clergy.

Each could potentially rule society by itself, but they more often rule in combination—and now you have an effective way to describe these combinations, or even to invent new ones!

This model allows you to very quickly sketch out the main political actors in your story and the power relations between them. Using it, you can very quickly create clarity out of a vague muddle of initial ideas.

Next chapter, we will look at the final piece of the puzzle: once a ruler is in power, how does she *stay* there? And how, and when, does she lose power?

Chapter 15: Selectorate Theory

By now, you have a lot of powerful tools to work with. You can set the base conditions with the right social order, you can look at your four Regime Actors and decide which are on top, and you can determine their stability (or lack of same!) with the Tripod of Power.

But these are all structural issues. We still need a way to tell how *individuals* gain or lose power—because that will be the heart of your story.

And that's the tricky bit. There are dozens of potential combinations of Regime Actors! And each of them results in a different kind of polity, which could have very different routes to power: democracies, dictatorships, aristocracies, and more. Does an author need to become an expert in all of them to write good political conflict?

Not necessarily. A good starting point would be a general theory of how regime leaders stay in power or get overthrown—simple enough to be easily applied to your story, flexible enough to be relevant to ancient kingdoms, modern democracies, and everything in between.

Fortunately, there is such a theory, developed by Bruce Bueno de Mesquita and his collaborators, and known in comparative politics as selectorate theory. It looks like this:

Winning Coalition

Selectorate

Residents
(disenfranchised)

Okay. Now what does all that mean?

Imagine a Kingdom of Crelia. Its king, Rothgar the VIII, rules over a strong aristocracy headed by nine barons, not all of whom like him very much, and a much larger pool of powerless peasants who pretty much have to suffer whatever comes. Rothgar doesn't have to worry much about what the peasants think; but he must pay attention to the barons, because if enough of them turned against him,

Rothgar could be overthrown and beheaded. Fortunately, he doesn't have to keep all of them happy all the time— just a fraction of them, let's say four. Their strength, plus his own, are enough to keep the other five barons in check.

To keep his supporters happy, therefore, King Rothgar keeps their taxes somewhat lower than the other five barons, gives them more privileges at court, and sets royal policy to favor their interests over those of the five other barons, to some degree. (The peasants, needless to say, get milked for all that Rothgar and the barons can get.)

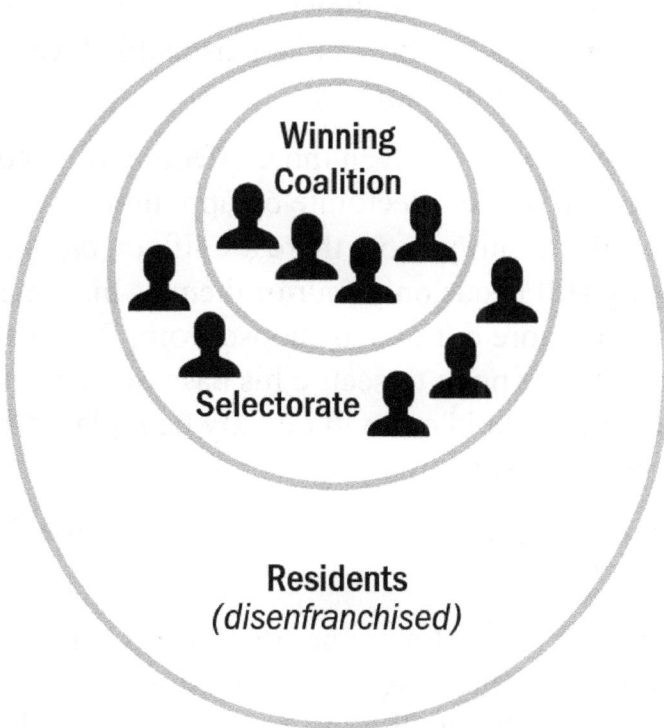

In terms of selectorate theory, the peasants (Residents) have no role in choosing the king. The nine barons, on the other hand, make up the *selectorate*—the group of people with the right, or the power, to influence the selection of king. The selectorate is the outer circle; the inner circle, on the other hand, is the winning coalition, the four barons who make up Rothgar's chief supporters.

Rothgar's survival depends on maintaining his winning coalition. But he need not keep the *same* four barons; indeed, his main leverage over them is the threat of replacing a pushy baron with one of the other five barons in the selectorate. That threat allows him to keep the expense of maintaining his allies down to a reasonable level, so he can keep more taxes to himself.

His threat would be even more effective if he could expand the size of the selectorate by appointing five or six peasants to the nobility. Now there are fifteen barons total, and the king still needs only four of them as his supporters. With so many more options to choose from, Rothgar need pay a much lower price to secure his base of support. Any baron that tries to hold out will quickly be replaced by a more cooperative rival.

However, suppose that there are not nine total barons but only six?

Then, each of the four supporter barons is in a powerful position; the king will have a much harder time replacing them individually, and has no way to replace them all. They can then extort a heavy price for their support, perhaps so heavy that the king's own revenue is

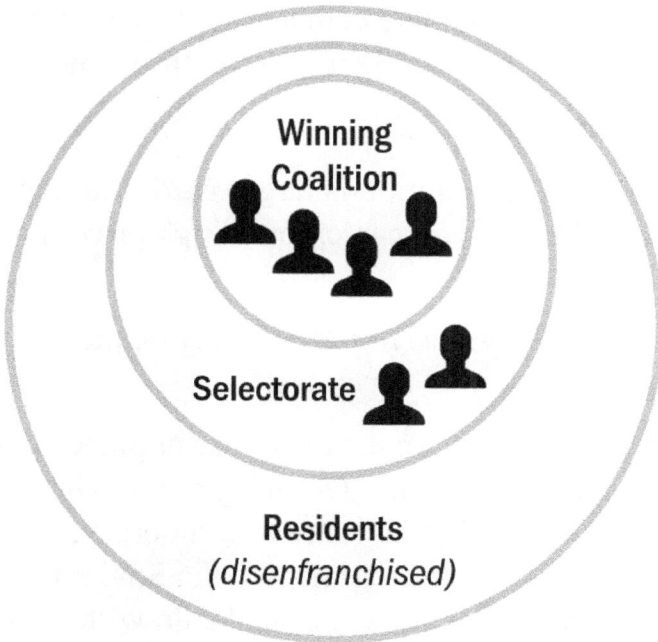

Winning
Coalition

Selectorate

Residents
(disenfranchised)

squeezed and he loses power over time. The same would be true if the king suddenly needed seven barons out of nine, instead of just four. (The country, needless to say, will suffer as spending on public goods drops off a cliff.)

And what if Rothgar cannot keep his supporters happy? They might throw their support to a challenger, Edwina—which might result in civil unrest, a bloodless coup, or even a nasty civil war.

Perhaps Edwina could put together a large enough winning coalition from all the members of the selectorate who were left out of Rothgar's coalition, along with a few of Rothgar's supporters who decide to betray him. If she can swing it, she could kick Rothgar out (or lock him in a dungeon, or cut off his head!), and take over as Queen.

Naturally, Edwina had better make it worth the while of her supporters, or *she* might lose her throne next!

Here's the general rule:

■ If the winning coalition is large *relative to the size of the selectorate*, it can extort a high price for its support.

■ If it is small *relative to the selectorate*, the ruler can keep more revenue for himself.

At the limit, if you make the entire populace part of the selectorate while only requiring a tiny winning coalition (for example with a strict meritocracy, or an authoritarian party-based regime like the Soviet Union), then your supporters will have to make do with meager benefits indeed.

Conversely, if your winning coalition must include the entire selectorate, they'll be able to milk you dry, or replace you with someone else.

Therefore:

■ The ruler has an interest in *expanding* the selectorate to cover a larger part of the population.

■ The existing selectorate members have an interest in *restricting* its size.

■ The ruler has an interest in *reducing* the necessary size of the winning coalition.

■ The selectorate would want to *increase* the size of the winning coalition.

You can see these dynamics play out in the political struggles over extending the right to vote. In the United States, for example, it was originally the case that only property-owning freemen could vote, about six percent of the population. (Government policy thus tended to favor the landowning class.)

Over time, the right to vote was slowly extended to most white men, then most men, then most adults. At each step, some who already had the vote feared that their interests would be harmed by the new voters, and fought bitterly against their inclusion.

And at each step, the size of the winning coalition grew along with that of the selectorate, and government policy thus changed to benefit larger and larger portions of the total populace.

Democracy

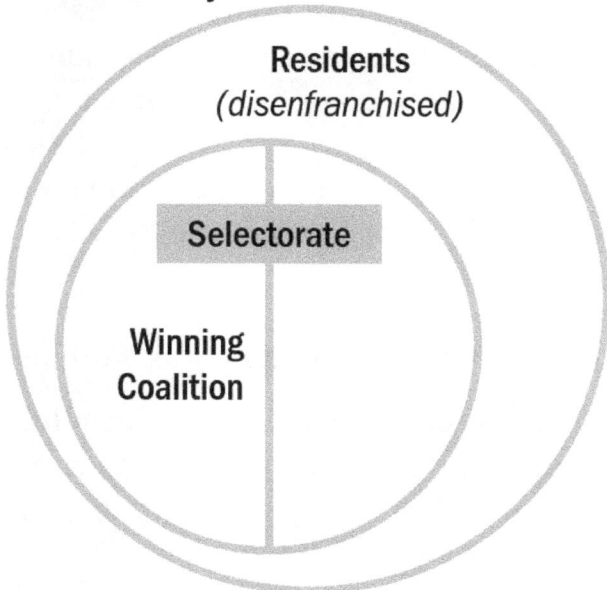

The previous paragraph is crucial.

When the winning coalition is small, it can be bought off with policies that benefit only a few powerful people, even if those policies harm the populace at large (as they often do; it is easy to tax the populace and enrich a handful of supporters).

But as the winning coalition grows, relative to the populace as a whole, it becomes more likely that policies benefiting the winning coalition will also benefit the populace in general. *This*, argues selectorate theory, is the main reason that democracies tend to be better-run (on average) than dictatorships—the ruler must set policies that benefit (or *supposedly* benefit) 50 percent of active voters at a minimum, instead of a small handful of powerful nobles, generals, or businessmen.

The model can fit any regime you imagine. Communism? The Communist Party membership was quite large, compared to the size of the Politburo; regime figures could be replaced easily, and often were. Banana republic? The key figures are the generals and the main business leaders, who are hard to replace and thus demand a high price for their support.

So what does selectorate theory do for us worldbuilders?

It allows us to zero in on the key political figures keeping our rulers in power. And *that* makes us ask what these figures want, whether they are likely to get it, and what they will do to the ruler if they don't.

Can anyone say "story conflict"?

Exercise

1. Spend five minutes thinking about your setting; then list all the kinds of people who have any influence at all on who the leader is. Are they powerful generals? Wealthy merchants? Priests? Voters in a democracy? Voters in an oligarchy or stratified society? Local nobles? Regional governors? Board directors or shareholders of a corporation? This is the selectorate.

1. Of all those people, what is the minimum level of support a leader would need to stay in power? How many different ways are there to put together such a winning coalition?

2. What could a leader offer his/her coalition members to keep them loyal? How could the leader threaten them?

3. If a coalition member is disloyal, how easily could the member be replaced with another member of the selectorate?

4. If the selectorate is unhappy with the leader, how easily could a new winning coalition be built behind someone else?

5. How might policies that favor the winning coalition harm people outside of it? (For example, tax the populace and give a subsidy to coalition members.) How might potential policies to benefit the populace harm members of the coalition, and thus be rejected? (For example, build a port that would make grain cheaper when your supporters are rich landowners who sell grain.)

6. How might new classes of people join the selectorate? (For

example, give women the right to vote.) Who would benefit from such a change? Who would be harmed?

7. How could existing classes of people lose their place in the selectorate? (For example, a democracy becomes a dictatorship; or powerful religious leaders are displaced by a religious purge.) Who would benefit from such a change?

8. How might the leader need fewer supporters, or more supporters?

9. Looking at all the possibilities for conflict that you listed above, which has the most resonance for the story you want to tell?

Further Reading

Bruce Bueno de Mesquita and Alastair Smith, *The Dictator's Handbook: Why Bad Behavior is Almost Always Good Politics*. (This is the mass-market discussion of selectorate theory. It contains a lot of vivid examples from real life, in a range of contexts. Highly recommended.)

Conclusion
(But Wait, There's More!)

You made it. Congrats!

You started this book wanting to learn how to create more awesome political conflicts in your worldbuilding. You now have several powerful tools to do that:

- Class conflict and social orders

- The Tripod of Power

- Regime Actors and polities

- Selectorate theory

At this point, let me repeat something I said at the very beginning:

The point is not to be realistic for its own sake. You can change anything you want, if it helps you write the story you want to tell.

That said… do you think that you can use these tools to write *new* stories? Cooler stories?

I do.

Stories that go beyond the clichés of princesses, peasants, and Robin Hood.

Stories where a reader isn't going to throw down your book and say, "This is stupid!"

Stories where the conflicts are important, the stakes are high, and everything is tied deeply, fundamentally, back into the decisions you made when building your world.

And best of all…

You might use the tools from this book. You might use the brainstorming exercises from this book (and you should!). But the story itself will come from *you*.

It won't be an unconscious rehash of the last ten TV shows you saw, or the last twenty books you read. Because you'll have the chance to build your world from the ground up—with your key story conflicts in mind from the beginning.

So go build!

Actually, keep reading for a bit… and *then* go build.

This book is the first in a larger series, *Politics for Worldbuilders*. While this one gave you focused, powerful insights into who rules societies, the next book in the series will take a closer look at how they rule.

Earlier, we briefly discussed topics like taxation and the projection of administrative power. These are part of the larger category of "state capacity"—or, to put it more bluntly, government control.

In the next volume, *Tyranny for Worldbuilders*, strategies of control take center-stage. Instead of asking who is in charge, we'll look at the common constraints and challenges that *any* would-be ruler must face in imposing her will on the hapless peasants, and the common techniques for dealing with these challenges.

And just like in this volume, we'll be focusing on the key conflict points and how you can use them in worldbuilding.

And believe me, can you ever!

For a single example, the movie *Enemy of the State* was an early look at the implications of total government surveillance. The government's desire for unlimited monitoring, its technological capacity to carry it out, and the political conflict around its use drove the entire plot of the movie.

In the following sneak preview of *Tyranny for Worldbuilders*, you'll be introduced to the fundamental concept behind the need for surveillance: *legibility*.

And it goes far beyond mere surveillance.

Suppose you wake up one day to find that you are the new king of your very own state.

After a moment of shock, you start to think about all the cool things you can do now—the laws you can pass, the taxes you can collect, the armies you can raise. But then you realize that even if you pass a law, you don't know if people will follow it; even if you impose taxes, you don't know if people will pay them; even if you raise an army, you don't know whether it will remain loyal.

In short, sitting in your palace at the center of your new domain, your first problem—maybe your most severe problem—is being able to perceive what people are doing.

There are several strategies you could use in response. For example:

- You could appoint trusted subordinates to carry out your will and enforce your laws—if you have such trusted subordinates!

- You could impose head taxes or customs duties at the city gates or other travel bottlenecks, so people passing through will be unable to avoid them.

- You can pay your military most of your income, so they have little incentive to rebel.

But each of these approaches has limits on its own. A more ambitious strategy, used by practically all states throughout history, is to deliberately increase the populace's *legibility*: the degree to which its activity can be monitored.

The classic discussion of legibility is by James C. Scott, across several of his books—most directly, *Seeing*

Like a State and *The Art of Not Being Governed*. In a nutshell, states force changes in their subjects' behavior in order to more easily monitor and control them.

One example is having people carry an identity card; in our modern society, this is convenient for businesses as well as governments. But back in the days when most people lived in the same village all their lives, and knew each other intimately, the only purpose of identity papers was for the traveling government official to know whether you had paid your taxes this year.

More drastic examples include:

- German "scientific forestry," in which a complex forest ecosystem was demolished and replaced with a monocrop of elm trees, grown in carefully measured rows and columns, so that the lumber yield from the forest would be predictable (in theory);

- the frequent practice in Southeast Asia of forcing your peasants to live in your capital city, so that their behavior can be easily observed;

- demanding that they all plant wheat, which can be easily assessed and taxed just before harvest, and making it a crime to grow potatoes (which grow underground and can easily be concealed from the taxman); and

- forcing people to take on last names, to make censuses easier and to better distinguish "William of Hole-in-the-Wall" and "William of Top-of-the-Hill" in the official records.

Writing in 1951, Hannah Arendt imagined with horror what Soviet intelligence would be able to do if they possessed a social-network graph of their captive populace, the better to monitor dissidents and punish them, their families, and everyone they ever knew. That is a key goal of legibility.

(Of course, we today have obligingly entered ourselves into such a social-network graph, providing it with intimate data about our lives that any intelligence service would drool over—to our growing sorrow. We also carry tracking devices in our cars and on our persons! Truly, we are the most legible generation in all of history.)

On the flip side, some people strive to make themselves less legible to the state, to evade its control. This is one reason why merchants, nomadic communities, and "barbarians" are typically viewed with suspicion by "official" society, since their capital is easily moved and they are hard to tax or control.

In general, however, the basic rule is more legibility equals more control.

This is not just true with states. One of the enduring problems of business organization is how to make sure that one's employees are doing what they are being paid to do. Production quotas were an early (and crude) mechanism to monitor employees; nowadays, employers often use video cameras, monitoring software on work computers, and the like.

You can even see this concept on the personal level: think of the controlling husband who demands that his wife use only a credit card that he has the password for, the better to control her spending. (Or think of a controlling wife, for that matter.)

You can see how the theme of legibility can be a rich vein of conflict for fiction!

An especially important spur to social conflict is when a new technology, or form of magic, or type of organization such as a police force or intelligence service, disrupts the status quo of legibility and suddenly makes people easier or harder to monitor. This can be an advanced technology for tracking people's movements or even their thoughts; or it could be something as mundane (to our eyes) as the first census in a country, in which the populace suddenly is categorized and sorted by the regime to enable better control.

As an example, the Biblical figure of King David carries out a census and is said to have sinned grievously by doing so—so much so that the realm is punished with a divine death plague. The political scientist in me wonders whether this "death plague" is a coded reference to violent popular resistance to the census; in Southeast Asia, as Scott notes, the very first objective of rioting peasants often was not to lynch the local landlord (that came second), but to burn down the government's records office.

Conversely, think of the heartburn that some governments are feeling over the growth of cryptocurrencies, which aspire to be completely untraceable and thus beyond the reach of taxation authorities.

In your fiction, the interplay between legibility and obscurity can drive compelling conflicts with the state, or with an employer, or a local mafia boss, or even within families. For states, the topic has implications for taxation, how armies are raised and led, and a host of other details. Again, a single fundamental constraint gives rise to many rich problems, all of which can be of service in your writing.

If you liked this preview of *Tyranny for Worldbuilders*, go to our website at https://lagrangebooks.com/ and sign up to be notified when it's published, along with future volumes of *Politics for Worldbuilders*. Your email will never be given away or sold, and you won't be spammed.

Did you use this book to write a cool story? Submit it to Lagrange Books for publication!